Girls just wanna have CLEAN!

Meredith® Books
Des Moines, Iowa

Girls Just Wanna Have Clean!

Editor: Vicki L. Christian
Contributing Writer: Diane Witosky
Graphic Designer: Craig Hanken, Bethanie Aswegan—Studio P2
Copy Chief: Terri Fredrickson
Publishing Operations Manager: Karen Schirm
Edit and Design Production Coordinator: Mary Lee Gavin
Editorial Assistants: Kaye Chabot, Kairee Windsor
Marketing Product Managers: Aparna Pande, Isaac Petersen, Gina Rickert,
    Stephen Rogers, Brent Wiersma, Tyler Woods
Book Production Managers: Pam Kvitne, Marjorie J. Schenkelberg,
    Rick von Holdt, Mark Weaver
Contributing Copy Editor: Carol Boker
Contributing Proofreaders: Kenya McCullum, Mindy Kralicek, Sue Fetters
Cover Illustration: Bonnie Dain
Indexer: Jana Finnegan

Meredith® Books
Executive Director, Editorial: Gregory H. Kayko
Executive Director, Design: Matt Strelecki
Executive Editor/Group Manager: Denise L. Caringer

Publisher and Editor in Chief: James D. Blume
Editorial Director: Linda Raglan Cunningham
Executive Director, Marketing: Jeffrey B. Myers
Executive Director, New Business Development: Todd M. Davis
Executive Director, Sales: Ken Zagor
Director, Operations: George A. Susral
Director, Production: Douglas M. Johnston
Business Director: Jim Leonard

Vice President and General Manager: Douglas J. Guendel

Meredith Publishing Group
President: Jack Griffin
Senior Vice President: Bob Mate

Meredith Coporation
Chairman and Chief Executive Officer: William T. Kerr
President and Chief Operating Officer: Stephen M. Lacy

In Memoriam: E.T. Meredith III (1933-2003)

All of us at Meredith® Books are dedicated to providing you with information and ideas
to enhance your home. We welcome your comments and suggestions. Write to us at:
Meredith Books, Home Decorating and Design Editorial Department, 1716 Locust St.,
Des Moines, IA 50309-3023.

If you want to order any of the titles below, call Meredith at 1-800-678-8091, write to us at
the address above, or visit us at meredithbooks.com:

- **Clutter Cutters—Store It With Style**
- **301 Stylish Storage Ideas**
- **Bathroom Idea File**
- **Kitchen Idea File**
- **Remodeling Idea File**

Ok, Let's Face It ...

* * *

We all love to have a sparkling, clean, well-organized place. But we don't want to spend our lives doing it.

I'd much rather spend time with friends, take a walk, pet my puppy, shop, or have fun with my significant other. But that doesn't make me a naughty girl.

Women who don't want to spend hours each week cleaning shouldn't feel inferior to their tidy Moms. Or less fulfilled than those frighteningly organized women who clip every single coupon and do isometric exercises to trim their backsides in grocery store checkout lines.

It just makes us girls who wanna have clean without putting a bunch of time and energy into it. (So we can spend the rest of our lives having FUN.)

That's where this book comes in. It has hundreds of cleaning and organizing tips to make your place sparkle in no time. Before you know it, you'll be all cleaned up with somewhere to go.

Enjoy!

Jodi Christean

Editor

Table of Contents

Table of Contents

Chapter 5–All Systems Go

Chapter 6–Talk Clean To Them

Chapter 7–Home Safe

Chapter 8–Emergency Cleaning Plan

Girls Just Wanna Have Clean

COMING CLEAN

1

Like your 9th-grade teacher probably told you a million times, if you don't have a plan, you plan to fail. Well, I'm not that fatalistic, but I've found, through messes you don't even want to know about, that you need to have a cleaning plan before you start. Here's your chance to discover what to do when, and how to do it so it fits your lifestyle. We show you all the tools and equipment—and how to clean FAST. We also offer thrifty hints for cheapskates (like me) who like to keep cleaning savings in a special little kitty to spend on fun.

Coming Clean

It's Your Party
✳ ✳ ✳

Your cleaning party, that is. So you get to decide how you want to do it and what works best for your schedule. Depending on your lifestyle, you may find it easier to do the basics daily and leave big chores for a weekend.

If you'd rather have weekends frcc for fun timc, do onc room or chore every day, in addition to daily chores.

Reserve a block of time for the huge jobs, such as attics, basements, or garages. Luckily, they only need cleaning about once a year.

(If you get tired, they're quiet places where you can take a quick nap with the best cookies in the pantry. Leave the plain sandwich ones for the kids to gobble up. They don't get the difference anyway.)

Do Daily or Weekly

Keeping public areas—living and dining rooms—neat may be important to you. You may be less vigilant about your bedroom and hobby space—places where guests won't see the mess, if there is one. (I'd do most of this weekly, but you already know all about my priorities!)

- Pick up items lying around and put them away in their right places.
- Empty the garbage.
- Make the beds.
- Wash the dishes and unload the dishwasher.
- Clean the toilet and the bathroom.
- Clean the pet dishes and the floor around them.
- Change litter boxes if you have cats (make sure you have one litter box per cat).
- Vacuum rugs, but don't move all the furniture around every time—twice a year is fine for this.

Coming Clean

- Dust (maybe not all those little tiny things, just around them).
- Water plants—better yet, get artificial ones, and you won't have to water anything at all.
- Sweep and mop the noncarpeted floors.
- Change bed sheets (this is super important because if you don't, you'll get dust mites that eat and live off human skin flakes and look terrifying even when not magnified to 200 times their size).

Do Monthly

- Thoroughly clean each room.
- Clean mirrors, telephones, stereos, picture frames.
- Clean the oven.
- Wash some of the windows (don't do all of them at once—rotate this job so you don't get window elbow, which could impair your shopping elbow).

Do Occasionally (one to three times a year)

- Defrost the fridge.
- Clean mineral deposits out of the coffeemaker and the steam iron.
- Wash the blankets.
- Clean the closets (you may be able to cut your taxes by donating items to the Salvation Army).

Do Yearly

- Move heavy furniture and clean behind and under it.
- Wash the walls.
- Shampoo carpets/drapes.
- Clean the filter in the stove exhaust fan.
- Oil sliding door tracks.
- Clean light fixtures.

Don't, Don't, Don't
* * *
Routinely clean up a family member's same mess time after time. (See how to avoid doing this in Chapter 6.)

Attack dust bunnies daily (they're such gentle souls).

Look under anyone's bed— what you don't see won't hurt you.

Spend days turning cans in the kitchen cabinets the same way, so the labels show at the same angle.

Invite spur-of-the-moment company home if your kids have been home all day during vacation. (My sister did this once and found her three teens and the dog gathered in the dining room, all eating out of a huge saucepan of cold, leftover macaroni. The dog was on top of the table, but at least the kids were seated in chairs.)

Give in to your significant other's demands to realphabetize your spices daily.

Give in to your significant other's demands to scrub around the faucets with an old toothbrush and scouring kitchen cleaner.

Attention, Cheapskates!

✳ ✳ ✳

Ok, now I know you're listening. Read on to save while you suds.

Buy cleaning supplies at the popular dollar stores that are popping up all over the country. Just be sure to check the expiration dates.

Use baking soda on a damp cloth for a nonabrasive cleaner for porcelain-topped surfaces. It's cheaper.

Use ½ cup vinegar mixed with 1 tablespoon salt as a substitute cleaner for copper and brass. It's less expensive than commercially prepared cleaners.

Make your own polishing cloths from old woolen socks or T-shirts.

Rent—don't buy—such cleaning machinery as large wet/dry vacuums or floor polishers. They're expensive, hard to transport, and require lots of maintenance.

Cut cleaning costs by doing it yourself, with your family's help. Maid services can cost up to $150 monthly.

Shop for bargains on brooms and vacuums. Ask for discounts on expensive items such as vacuums.

Keep your color palette light. White fixtures, tubs, toilets, and sinks cost less than those in colors and are actually easier to clean.

What Not to Save Money On
✶ ✶ ✶

I've learned these the hard way, saving a few cents by yanking and tearing. So don't scrimp on the following.

Toilet paper: My sister once got some so cheap that there were small wood-like splinters in it—YOW!

Plastic wrap: This can keep you wrestling for hours, occasionally wounding yourself with the forked fake aluminum edge that's supposed to cut the wrap but doesn't. You'll end up with a tangled web that will test the patience of your family members.

Garbage bags: The culprits are the really thin ones that even paper can poke holes through. Worse yet, they lack ties, handles, or any way at all to draw the top together over the trash. (This ensures a mad search through your junk drawers for rubber bands. This can injure your self-esteem. Just say no.)

Vehicular Vanity

You don't want to live in a mess, so why drive in a

messy car? Get an automotive trash caddy and empty it daily. Spring for a car air freshener too. Vanilla is good.

The Right Stuff
* * *

If you've ever tried to sweep with a child's toy broom purchased by mistake (OK, I'll admit I was desperate), you know how important it is to have the right cleaning items to do the job.

Get this equipment and go get 'em:

A Well-Stocked Cleaning Caddy

Buy a sturdy plastic cleaning caddy. (No, it has nothing to do with golf. You won't even have to watch the movies every man loves to recite in their entirety: "Caddyshack" and "Caddyshack II.")

Next, stock your caddy with cleaning supplies and tools.

If you live in a two-story house, you may want a second caddy upstairs. Keep brooms and mops upstairs as well, unless you're into aerobics. (Then you could burn calories running up and down the stairs to ward off the effects of those morning Danishes. Love 'em!)

Put area-specific supplies in the bathroom and kitchen. Store cleaning supplies behind locked doors—out of the kids' reach.

Don't have a different cleaning product for every task. Get a multipurpose one. (Remember how Grandma or Great-Grandma used lye soap for everything and lived to tell the tale?)

You Get to Go Shopping
* * *

Sure, it's for cleaning supplies, but it's shopping.

Coming Clean

Buy That Bleach

Dilute 1 part bleach with 4 parts water for general cleaning and disinfecting (including toilet bowls).

A mild bleach solution (1 tablespoon to 1 quart water) will kill bacteria; use stronger solutions for whitening.

Before you apply bleach, test areas for colorfastness.

Don't keep bleach and water solutions for more than 24 hours.

An Ode to Bleach

1. You smell clean.

2. You remind me of my Mom cleaning house, when I was little and there were so many possibilities.

3. You make things whiter and better.

4. Girls just gotta have plenty of bleach.

Cop a Cleanser

Choose a nonabrasive one (no grits) for general cleaning. Buy a heavy-duty one for tough stains and rust.

Add Ammonia

Household ammonia is a strong dirt cutter (followed by detergent, then borax).

Use diluted ammonia to clean appliances, glass surfaces, range hoods and filters, and windows. Always dilute 1 part ammonia with 4 parts water.

Breathing ammonia fumes can damage lungs; open the windows for fresh air before using.

IMPORTANT: Never mix ammonia and bleach—it creates toxic gas.

OK for Oil Soap

Use oil soap to clean wood cabinets and other woods, such as paneling.

Bows to Baking Soda

Baking soda is a great natural deodorizer for many areas. Put it in refrigerators, suitcases, closets, and dresser drawers.

Use mildly abrasive baking soda to clean sinks, bathtubs, and countertops by sprinkling it on damp surfaces and scrubbing with a damp sponge.

Make it into a paste like peanut butter for added cleaning power.

Sprinkle it on damp spots, spills, or greasy spots on carpets and rugs. Let it dry and vacuum the residue.

To clear slow drains, pour 1 cup baking soda down the drain. Slowly add 1 cup white vinegar. (Use ½ cup for small sinks.) Cover with a stopper, let the mixture fizz for 5 minutes, and flush with a gallon of hot water if your pipes are PVC (polyvinyl chloride).

Use the baking soda/vinegar combo just described for cleaning scorched stainless-steel (not the aluminum) pots, and removing baked-on foods from oven-safe dishes.

"A" for Antibacterial Soap

Wash your hands with it before and after handling raw meat, poultry, and eggs—or when your family is ill. (One down is bad, two is worse, and three is time to order Pizza Hut delivery.)

Get Window Cleaner

Window cleaner is great, all-purpose stuff. It smells good too.

Use it for windows, glass tops, mirrors, polishing chrome fixtures, and cleaning cooktops.

Dash for Detergent

Detergent is a good all-purpose cleaner when dissolved in warm water. Rinse surfaces well.

To avoid suds, fill the cleaning bucket with water; stir in detergent.

Go for Gloves

Gloves protect delicate hands from heavy work. They also help your manicure last longer. Non-latex gloves are also available if you're allergic to latex.

Do Dry Mops

Dry mops have shaggy heads that can be removed and laundered. Spray the mop head with a cleaner for attracting dust, mop the surface, and then shake the mop outside to remove dust.

To wash your mop, put the mop head in a mesh laundry bag. Machine wash it in cold water.

Fetch a Feather Duster

Dusters safely clean lampshades, light fixtures, delicate collectibles, and pieces of art.

An added plus: You'll feel so dainty and feminine while you use it.

Clean Again, Naturally
* * *

It's thrifty to use natural cleaning products such as lemons, salt, and vinegar. They work best for routine cleaning, not heavy grime. (But I know you'd never let anything get that dirty. I certainly never have. Not!)

Let's Get Lemons

The natural acid of lemons cuts through mineral buildup and tarnish, but not through heavy grease. Fresh lemons or freshly squeezed lemon juice work better than bottled lemon juice.

Coming Clean

To remove tarnish from copper, dip half a lemon in salt, rub it on the surface, rinse, and dry.

Freshen a garbage disposal by cutting up lemons and running them through it.

Pass the Salt

Although salt is more abrasive than baking soda, it will scratch only the most delicate surfaces.

Sprinkle it on dirty areas and then rub the area gently with a damp cloth.

Remove hard-water spots from vases with ⅓ cup salt and 2 tablespoons white vinegar. Apply to the film. Let the paste set for 20 minutes. Scrub to loosen the film, and rinse vase well.

To remove rust from metal, use ¼ cup salt mixed with 1 tablespoon lemon juice. Scrub the surface of the metal with this mixture, rinse with warm water, and buff dry.

Salt is absorbent—you can clean up many spills by sprinkling it on the spot. Let it stand for 1 hour, and then vacuum.

WOW for White Vinegar

Vinegar cuts through soap film and mineral deposits. It's an excellent rinse because it won't leave a sticky residue.

(And white vinegar isn't prejudiced against other styles and colors of vinegars. You can even put them next to each other in the cabinet and you won't hear a peep of complaint from any of them.)

For a fresh scent when you clean with vinegar, add a few drops of essential oils from a health food or crafts store. Lemon, lavender, pine, and mint work well.

You can also dissolve stubborn hard-water stains with vinegar. For mineral buildup on faucets and around drains, soak a cloth in vinegar, lay it on the stain, and then leave it for an hour. Scrub the deposits with a soft brush. Finally, rinse the surfaces thoroughly.

Be Kind to Your Cleansers

✳ ✳ ✳

Treat your household cleansers gently and properly, and they'll work better for you.

Open packages correctly. (Usually I'm in a hurry and poke a knife into the box somewhere, which isn't good, because the stuff dribbles out inappropriately. It irritates other family members too.)

Tear closure tabs or slots as the directions indicate. This helps keep your cleaning products fresh.

Close cleaning packages after each use. This preserves products, prevents spills, and limits moisture pickup and clumping inside packages.

Be sure to close all cleaning containers properly, especially the ones labeled as "childproof."

Store products in a cool, dry place, locked away from the kids. Temperatures can alter the effectiveness of many cleaning products.

Life on the Shelf

Many commercial household cleaners have unlimited shelf lives—just check the label on the product to be sure.

Some cleaners—with sodium hypochlorite (bleach)—lose strength and effectiveness over time. (Kind of like some of those ill-fated relationships I've had in the past.)

Store your cleaning products between 50 and 70 degrees F. Homemade products with baking soda, borax, essential oils, liquid soap, detergent, and water have indefinite shelf lives if tightly sealed.

(They may even outlive styrofoam, who knows?)

Discard home-recipe cleaning products that have any food ingredients, such as herbal teas or yogurt, immediately after you use them.

Create a Home Cleaning Center That Rocks

Buy a wall rack to hang all of your brooms, mops, rags, sponges and dustpans.

Use baskets, bins, and caddies to store all of your products and supplies. You can usually purchase inexpensive ones at home discount stores or dollar stores—some even come in fun colors, like hot pink.

Be sure to safely store all cleaning supplies out of your kids' reach.

Put daily, weekly, and monthly tasks on a small bulletin board in your kitchen or cleaning supply pantry. And DO get your family to help you. After all, they live there too!

Keep a supply checklist, and post it in your cleaning center. When a product runs low, put it on the list so you can pick it up the next time you shop. Then, no one in your family will ever have the excuse not to clean because you're out of a product.

Rooms with a (Clean) View
✳ ✳ ✳
Blast the Bath

Have everyone in your family at least rinse the tub after each use. It takes just a few seconds, especially if they use a water tumbler, fill it with water, and pour the water on the tub surfaces.

This will keep soap film and hard-water deposits from ever forming in the first place.

Coming Clean

Stash a spray bottle with an all-in-one window and surface cleaner in the bathroom. Another plus to these products is that they're nonabrasive, so they won't scratch surfaces.

Put some extra rolls of paper towels under the sink for quick and easy cleanup (should any family member have the unexpected urge to do that).

Keep extra rolls of toilet paper under the bathroom sink or in the vanity. (This will stop those plaintive cries— "Mooom, can you bring me some toilet paper"—that tend to interrupt your day.)

For fine-finish faucets, apply silver polish, rinse thoroughly, and wipe dry. Shine brass faucets with rubbing alcohol.

Gently clean gold-plated faucets with warm sudsy water and rinse. Use undiluted bleach to remove pits and stains on porcelain.

Use special rust removers to clean rust stains. Avoid using products with bleach to remove rust stains, because they can intensify the color of the stains.

Replace worn bath mats, shower curtains, and liners. If you don't want your tub to look like a peculiar person uses it, avoid sticky grab holders like grinning frogs and dancing daisies.

Shower Power

Keep the shower doors and curtains open after each use to allow them to air-dry and to prevent any mildew from forming on surfaces.

For shower surfaces and glass doors, spray cleaner works well.

Towel dry shower walls after each use, or get a squeegee (such a fun word) to use after each shower.

Tidy the Toilets

Spray the toilet exterior with a general-purpose bathroom cleaner or a vinegar/water mixture.

Sanitize surfaces with antibacterial toilet cleaner or ¼ cup bleach to 1 gallon of water. (Or get those cool toilet cleaner things that make the water aqua. Kids like them.)

Conquer the Kitchen

Keep a spray bottle with a solution of 1 part bleach to 4 parts water or an all-purpose spray cleaner for quick and easy cleanups.

Wipe up spills right away, so they don't get harder to remove. (Letting them harden sometimes makes interesting flat, free-form sculptural shapes though.)

Line the tray beneath what you're cooking with foil, for easy cleanup. (Then you won't set off the smoke alarm when you cook, scaring family and guests.)

It's best to use products like sprays or gels on small areas, such as kitchen countertops. For cleaning larger areas, such as walls and floors, it's more efficient to use a powder or liquid cleaner mixed in a pail of water.

Unleash the power of your dishwasher. Use it to clean toys, knickknacks, oven vents, and light fixtures. If you're not sure if an item is dishwasher-safe, don't set the machine to dry, as drying is the harshest cycle.

To avoid bacteria that could make people sick, wash your hands thoroughly before and after handling food—particularly raw meat, poultry, eggs. (Or go to a clean restaurant several nights a week if you can afford it, and avoid the whole issue.)

Reused dishcloths are more germy than sponges. If cloths are machine-washed and dried after every use, they're cleaner than sponges, but who has time to do that?

Replace sponges frequently, or toss them into the dishwasher. Odor means bacterial contamination. (If you've smelled your teenage son's gym shoes lately, you know what I mean.)

Sanitize cutting boards with fresh bleach. (My favorite cleaning product does it again.) Buy hard maple, not soft wood. Sand to remove any scratches that harbor bacteria; oil to seal.

Use paper towels, not cloths or sponges, to wipe up meat juices.

Yearly, wipe out cabinets and install fresh shelf paper. (This is always fun, trying to measure it right and get it to fit. Now I see why the wine stains keep happening in my kitchen.)

Discard stale spices or any outdated items.

Clean the refrigerator and freezer regularly. (With the freezer, it's best to do this before the ice grows huge stalagmites that allow you to put in only a tiny entree.)

Vacuum the cooling coils under or behind the refrigerator, if you're feeling especially hardy.

Seasonal Sensations
✳ ✳ ✳
Spring Fling

Get organized to save time and energy. Go in and out of the house, looking at what you need to do, so you can prioritize projects. You might even want to make a list because it's always fun to cross out each thing after you do it—such a feeling of accomplishment. You could then divide your list into:

LARGE PROJECTS: Major bummer—half day or more.

MEDIUM PROJECTS: Minor bummer—two to three hours.

SMALL PROJECTS: No sweat—easy when you find a little time.

Face Floors and Walls

Mop and scrub floors and walls with a nonsudsing household ammonia or a cleaner safe for vinyl.

Bold in the Bedroom

Rotate and flip mattresses. (Unless you've really been working out, you might want to interrupt one of your family member's games of Nintendo to help you.)

Wash or dry clean the area rugs. Wash and/or wax floors.

Wash blankets or comforters or take them to the cleaners. (Dry cleaning adds up—investigate using coupons.)

Wash the mattress pad and the bed skirt. Hang pillows (minus their covers) outside in the sun and fresh air.

Use a soft cotton cloth or regular paper towels to clean any glass surfaces. Extra-absorbent paper towels can leave lint behind.

For artwork, spray glass cleaner on the cloth or regular paper towel instead of directly on the glass surface. This keeps the cleaning product away from the frame, so it won't seep onto the picture.

Master Main Living Areas

Deep-clean rugs or have the carpets professionally cleaned. Watch for coupons—often carpet cleaners give great spring discounts. Wash the baseboards and all of the moldings. Vacuum the upholstery and the draperies. (Try using headrest and armrest covers to protect the areas of your furniture that get the most concentrated wear.)

Dust and wax wood furniture. This isn't hard, and it's kind of fun, especially if you use a product with a fresh lemon or springtime scent.

Vacuum upholstered pieces, including under cushions and in crevices. (Watch not only for crumbs and empty candy wrappers, but for loose change you can put in your secret kitty to save and spend on something fun. And don't feel guilty—finders-keepers.)

Always use coasters under drinking glasses, plants, and cups. They help prevent water spots and rings on any wooden surface.

Walk the Deck

Clean your deck or porch. Decide if you need to reseal, stain, or paint it.

Clean and check concrete stoops for chips or cracks. Those can be nasty because ants like to crawl around in there.

Windows and Screens

Replace storm windows with clean screens. (Get out your portable boom box and play oldies or hip-hop music and sing. Make it look like fun and you may get your neighbors to help.)

Use cotton swabs or a soft toothbrush to clean corners. (Just remember not to reuse the toothbrush to brush your teeth and you'll be fine.)

Prepare to Plant

Bring out garden tools and potting supplies. Store snow shovels, salt, scrapers, etc.

Fun with Patio Furniture

Bring out, clean, and touch up deck, porch, or patio furniture, if it's stored.

Use outdoor spray enamel to touch up chips, or spray paint plastic furniture. (Think pink. Think purple. Surprise your neighbors.)

Welcome, Winter
* * *
Blowing Hot and Cold

Clean vents in the furnace and change the air filters in the central air units.

NOTE: If you're not sure how to do this, call a heating professional to do these tasks and thoroughly check your furnace.

If you use a humidifier in the winter, be sure to clean and maintain it. (You probably should use one—otherwise you could get dry skin and more wrinkles than you deserve!)

Change batteries in smoke and carbon monoxide detectors throughout the house.

Buy a fire extinguisher and learn how to use it. Also, show all your family members how to use it. If you're single, take it to your local fire department and see if there's a single fireman who can demonstrate. (My girlfriend met a very nice single man that way.)

Get Out of the Gutter

Clean gutters before winter and in the spring. Or have them professionally done (especially if heights give you the same feeling as watching the shower scene in "Psycho").

Wash all of the interior windows. Clean around the windowsills and frames.

Out and About

Clean and store any outside furniture, garden pots, plant pots, and tools. Be sure to also clean outdoor furniture cushions before storing them to prevent mildew.

Remove lint from the outdoor dryer exhaust tubes. Did you know, if you leave too much lint in your dryer trap, it can cause a fire? My realtor told me so, and I looked it up on the Web and it's true.

Don't Forget

Replace worn-out doormats to reduce the amount of tracked-in dirt and snow. (Put a mat at each entrance.)

This is a good time to reduce clutter in your closets. As you bring out winter clothing, be ruthless. If you haven't worn it for a season, consider donating it to such organizations as the Salvation Army or Goodwill.

Also check each item to see if you need to replace buttons or mend tears. Then launder the items or take them to the dry cleaners, if necessary.

Tackle Tough Tasks
* * *

Behind Closed Doors

Wipe off the inside of cabinets and drawers with all-purpose cleaner or white vinegar diluted in water. Rinse and let them dry.

Install shelf paper to preserve surfaces and for easier cleaning. Shelf paper comes in paper, vinyl or rubber cut to fit, self-adhesive vinyl, and low-tack self-adhesive vinyl.

Paper lining is inexpensive, but it can't be washed and needs to be replaced often.

Vinyl lining is inexpensive and washable, but may slide and bunch up. Ugh.

Love Those Laminates

Wipe laminates with all-purpose cleaner or white vinegar diluted in water, rinse, and dry with a clean cloth.

Disinfect surfaces with an antibacterial kitchen cleaner or 1 tablespoon bleach (Did I mention I love bleach?) diluted in 1 quart water. Clean the seams between the surfaces, where the doors meet edges of frames.

To clean stains, rub them with a paste of baking soda and water.

Doing Heavy Metal

Metal cabinets usually have an enamel finish, so they're cared for in the same way as painted cabinets (below).

Pamper Painted Cabinets

Painted cabinets and drawer fronts sealed with oil-based paint are more durable and scrubbable than latex-painted wood.

Wash painted cabinets with warm water and diluted all-purpose cleaner, wood cleaner, or white vinegar. Don't get the wood too wet. Rinse with a second cloth and clear water. Dry.

Wipe areas that may be contaminated with bacteria—that nasty stuff again—(like around handles) with an antibacterial kitchen cleaner or a solution of 1 tablespoon bleach to 1 quart water. (Bleach is good for so many things.)

If grease builds up (I can't believe it would in your kitchen, because it certainly doesn't in mine—oh, right), wipe the cabinet and drawer fronts with ammonia and water; then rinse with water. For stubborn stains, loosen the dirt with a paste of baking soda and water; rinse and dry.

Coming Clean

Abrasive cleaners or scouring pads scratch paint. So be kind to your cabinets and don't use them.

Working on Wood

Oil-soap wood cleaners work well. Frequently polish or wax wood cabinetry to keep from cracking (I mean, the wood from cracking, not you).

Disinfect surfaces with a diluted antibacterial cleaner without bleach. Wipe on and rinse with a clean, damp cloth. Dry with a third cloth. Work with the grain of the wood when cleaning.

Countertop Countdown

Antibacterial kitchen cleaners or mild bleach solutions help control bacteria.

Be careful with bleach solutions. They may alter countertop colors. Test first on inconspicuous spots. Rinse well.

Use separate cloths for cleaning, rinsing, and drying. Don't use dishcloths used on food, dishes, or hands to dry countertops. It could spread bacteria.

For greasy buildups, use a kitchen cleaner. If the surface is especially sticky (wonder who spilled?), rub it with a paste of baking soda and water; then rinse.

STOP–in the Name of Stains
✳ ✳ ✳
Food and Wine

You may want to check into the source of these wine stains. Could it be from an adult member of your household who was forced to watch "How the Grinch Stole Christmas" seven times in a row when a toddler was sick? Well, whoever is the culprit, blot the wine or food stain immediately, especially on porous materials, such as butcher block. Use an all-purpose cleaner with bleach; rinse well.

Newspaper Ink

To avoid this altogether, just keep newspapers or those free shopper publications off your kitchen counters. (Take a minute to sit down and read them and quit that multitasking.) Cleaners with bleach will remove the stains.

Package Ink

Ink from damp household packaging can stain; be cautious with laminate or solid-surface materials. Usually, you can remove these stains by using cleaners with bleach.

Bust the Rust

Cans and damp spots are rust culprits. When you cook, wipe up as you spill. Use an all-purpose cleaner with bleach and rinse well.

Scary Scorching

Scorching can be bad news, because it may be permanent. But you can try a cleaner with bleach. Use trivets, hot pads, wood cutting boards, or folded towels to protect laminates so this doesn't happen.

Rings Around the Rosey

Wipe up spills before they leave telltale water rings. Use a cleaner with bleach.

The File on Tile

Tile doesn't stain easily—grout does. Grout is also the area most likely to harbor bacteria (here we go again with that icky stuff).

Scrub grout with a mild bleach solution, or use a bleach pen found in the laundry section of some grocery stores and home discount centers. Don't use abrasive pads.

Some people say clean each grout crack between tiles

with a toothbrush—I think that's a little much. Use a commercial grout sealer to help prevent future stains.

Wonderful for Wood

Oiling wood countertops keeps them from drying out and seals surfaces. Wipe the wood with a light coat of mineral oil. Let the oil soak into the surface.

Don't use linseed or vegetable oils because they can become rancid.

Stone Soul

Wipe surfaces of stone, slate, granite, or concrete with warm, sudsy water and rinse thoroughly. You may use a mild bleach solution, but don't use an abrasive cleanser or scrub pads, which will scratch and damage the surface.

To remove stains, make a paste of baking soda and water or talcum powder mixed with a diluted solution of ammonia, bleach, or hydrogen peroxide. Gently scrub the spot with the paste and a soft brush. Rinse thoroughly. Several applications may be needed.

Ceilings and Moldings

Occasionally wipe these down using a broom covered with a soft, lint-free cloth. Or vacuum them with a soft brush attachment.

If ceilings need washing, use an all-purpose cleaner, or dilute 2 tablespoons white vinegar or ammonia in a quart of water and scrub one small section at a time. Rinse with clear water and a rag.

(WARNING: This is a major job, speaking from one who thought it could be done in a couple of hours while watching "The Way We Were" for the fourth time on my new DVD player.)

Tiles on Top

You can vacuum ceiling tiles with a brush attachment to remove dust. (I'm 5'2", so I hope you're taller and don't have to stand on a chair like I do.) Because of texture and color variations, dirt here isn't normally a problem. (Who's that tall to see it anyway?)

Any streaks from water damage do show, so it's best to just replace the whole tile. Or seal it with a stain-resistant sealer and then paint it. (Take heart: Doing one tile won't take nearly as much time as doing the whole ceiling, so you can count yourself lucky.)

Decorative Moldings

Clean any dusty trim with a vacuum brush attachment, feather duster, or a soft paintbrush.

Clean dirty molding with all-purpose cleaner; test it first in an inconspicuous spot. Mix 1 cup ammonia, ½ cup white vinegar, ¼ cup baking soda, and 1 gallon warm water. Pour part of the solution into a spray bottle. Spray and wipe in small sections. Rinse with clear water and wipe dry with a soft cloth.

For picture molding, which has a gap above it for picture hooks, use a new soft paintbrush to remove the dust. If the gap is grimy, dip a cotton swab in cleaning solution and clean. Rinse with a swab dipped in clear water. Swab dry.

A Fan of Fans?

Fan blades collect dust and grease because they draw air upward. This is especially true for kitchen fans.

Dust ceiling fans monthly with a long-handled feather duster or electrostatic duster.

Remove grease and grime from fans and blades with all-purpose cleaner on a rag.

Coming Clean

Electronic Equipment

Use dust covers when electronics are not in use to avoid frequent dusting.

Computer Casings

Wipe computers with a clean, soft cloth dampened in water, nonabrasive wipes, or lint-free cloths. Never use alcohol or ammonia products. And don't spray computer casings or screens, because it could cause permanent damage.

Wipe screens with a cloth dampened with some window cleaner. Be careful: Liquid spills may seriously harm computers.

Computer Mouse

(This mouse is the only kind I like in my house.)

To clean your mouse, use cotton swabs, isopropyl alcohol, and tweezers. Take your mouse apart. (He won't feel a thing, I promise.) Swab or lift out dust

particles regularly. Wipe the ball and rollers with alcohol.

Keyboards and CPUs

Use a mini vacuum to pull dust away from computer vents and surfaces. Also vacuum the mouse pad. (A mouse loves you when you help keep his pad clean.)

Cleaning DVDs and CDs

Wipe DVDs and CDs in a straight line from the center out—not in a circle, because this can scratch. Use a damp, lint free cloth.

Clean the optical mechanism inside a compact disc player with a CD lens cleaner monthly to remove dust.

Record Players and LPs

Cover the turntable and clean the stylus after each session with a stylus-cleaning brush.

Don't touch LP grooves— this can cause permanent scratches. Use isopropyl alcohol to clean the surface, wiping in a circle from center out with a soft, lint-free cloth. Gently pat dry with another soft cloth.

The Boob Tube

Dust the TV screen with a soft cloth or duster. Dampen a cloth with window cleaner to clean the screen and cabinet. Vacuum the vents monthly.

LCDs

Unplug the set before cleaning the screen. Dust by wiping the screen and cabinet with a soft cloth.

If the screen needs cleaning, use a clean, damp cloth—liquid or aerosol cleaners could cause damage. Rubbing or tapping the screen with a hard object could cause permanent damage.

Plasma

(I know this sounds scary, like blood, but it really isn't.)

Clean the coated flat glass screen with a slightly damp, soft cloth. Abrasive cleaners or solvents can damage the glass screens.

Video Recorders

Experts don't agree whether cleaning recorders monthly with a commercial cleaning tape and solvent removes dust, but could scratch your tapes. (If you worry about this, find some interesting hobbies.) Just keep the units covered when you're not using them.

Score with Your Floor
* * *
Use Protection

Use sturdy plastic rounds to securely cup furniture legs and protect your floor from scratches. For really heavy furniture, use soft, textured rounds to protect from dents.

Coming Clean

Felt Circles

You can use self-adhesive rounds on the feet of lightweight furniture pieces, like dining room chairs, to protect wood floors. Replace them when worn.

Color-Coded Plastic

Plastic squares are sold in dark and light tones to blend with wood floors, and be less noticeable. They're usually sold at hardware stores and home centers.

Carpet Keepers

Spiked rounds and squares can help protect your carpets from compression dents. Clear-acrylic forms blend with many carpet colors. Choose a shape to fit best under the legs of the furniture you're using in that room.

Screw-In Protectors

You can attach these to furniture pieces you frequently move around, such as dining room chairs. Choose smooth pads that won't scratch hard-surface floors.

Carpet Care
✳ ✳ ✳

Regular vacuuming helps protect carpeting. As dirt sifts between the fibers, it can damage carpets and make them look worn.

Frequent vacuuming, using quality filter bags, also reduces household allergens. Vacuum the main living areas, stairs, and high-traffic areas of your home at least twice a week, and more frequently if you have children or pets.

Put doormats on both sides of exterior doors to trap the dirt outside the house.

Sweep, shake, rattle and roll out rugs twice weekly, particularly during bad weather, when more dirt is tracked in.

To vacuum stairs, you need to have good balance. Start at the bottom and work up to avoid pressing dirt into carpeted steps.

Colorfast Carpet?

To test the colorfastness of your carpet, use a carpet scrap. Vacuum it; then dampen a cloth with carpet cleaner. Lay the cloth on the carpet scrap for an hour. Blot with a white cloth. If the cloth is stained with carpet dyes, don't use carpet cleaner.

Deep-Cleaning Carpet

Thoroughly clean your carpet every 12 to 18 months—more often in the high-traffic areas. Clean it two or three times a year if you have kids and pets or if you have a light-colored carpet.

Before you deep-clean your carpet, remove all of the furniture from the room and vacuum thoroughly.

Depending on how much time you have to dedicate to this task, you may want to use some money from your secret kitty to hire a professional carpet cleaning service instead.

Make sure the carpet dries completely within 24 hours to prevent mold growth. You can use fans to help dry it more quickly. Don't move the furniture back until the carpet is dry.

No Stain Shall Remain

With stains, time is of the essence. For liquids, blot up—never rub—as much moisture as possible, working inward from the outside of the stain.

For solid spills, use a spoon or dull knife to remove the excess before cleaning.

Don't overwet carpets. (Be sure to explain this thoroughly to your cats and dogs.) Excess moisture can permanently damage the carpet backing.

Commercial spot carpet cleaners can remove most types of stains. Oxygen cleaners are best to remove organic stains.

Detergent Solution

Here's a thrifty tip: You can make your own cleaner for carpet stains. Just stir 1 teaspoon of liquid dishwashing detergent into a quart of warm water. Add ¼ teaspoon white vinegar.

Let the solution sit on the stain for 10 minutes before you blot it carefully. If this doesn't work, try a commercial product made especially for carpet stains.

White Vinegar Solution

This solution is recommended by the Carpet and Rug Institute. Just mix 1 cup white vinegar with 2 cups of water, apply to the area, and blot it dry.

Carpet Stain Removal Guide
✳ ✳ ✳
Alcohol and Soft Drinks

(OK, who had the party when you weren't home?) First, apply a detergent stain-removal formula. Then rinse, blot dry or use a wet vacuum to dry the entire area that's affected.

If the stain still remains, try a vinegar cleaning solution.

Blood

(Who wasn't careful with that new razor?) Treat blood stains immediately for the best results. Apply cold water or club soda and blot with a clean cloth. (Then call 911— just kidding).

Coffee and Tea

Apply a detergent solution. Rinse and blot it dry. If the

Coming Clean

stain still remains, apply a spot carpet cleaner. Blot it dry or use a wet-dry vacuum cleaner.

Creative Crayon

(Wonder how on earth this happened and who did it? Perhaps a neighbor's evil child snuck in at night and drew all those colorful cartoons on your living room walls.)

Scrape off the excess crayon marks with a dull-edged knife or spoon. Use a spot carpet and upholstery cleaner or a citrus-based oxygen cleaner. Gently work it into the spot. Blot. If the stain remains, repeat the whole process.

Specialty crayons and art materials may require other treatments. (By this time, your family members who use these items inappropriately should have enough experience to paint an imitation of The Sistene Chapel.)

Plain Old Dirt

Allow the dirt or mud to dry completely. Scrape off as much as possible and vacuum the area. Apply a detergent solution. Blot dry and repeat.

Fat-based Stains

Butter on popcorn, gravy, or margarine can cause these. Use a dry-solvent spot cleaner (then cook low-cholesterol recipes and tell your family they'll feel much healthier).

Grease and Oil

Sprinkle the area with baking soda and let it sit for at least six hours. Vacuum it and then apply a spot cleaner. Rinse and blot or wet vacuum it dry.

Dumb Gum

Peel away what you can. You can harden gum by placing a bag of ice cubes over it so it'll be easier to remove.

Coming Clean

Next, chip the gum away with a spoon or knife. (If you can identify the family culprit who did this, perhaps they can join you in this process for quality bonding time together.)

Vacuum to remove the loosened gum. Spot clean the area with dry-solvent spot cleaner.

Paint

These stains can be hard to remove and may require professional treatment.

For acrylic and latex paint stains, spot clean them with a detergent solution while they're wet. If any color remains, dab the area gently with some rubbing alcohol.

For oil-based paint stains, sponge the area with odorless mineral spirits, but don't completely soak the carpet backing—it may cause damage.

Pet Stains

For the best results, clean up accidents as soon as possible. Try to absorb a fresh stain with paper towels, so it doesn't soak into the carpet or the upholstery.

If you find an accident later, you can still remove the odor. If it's solid waste, remove it with paper towels.

Then put a little water on the area and blot it. Next, dilute vinegar in a bottle and spray on the stain. Allow the spot to dry. This may remove the odor. If this doesn't work, sprinkle borax powder or baking soda on the area and let it dry for eight hours. Then vacuum.

Never rub a pet stain— it can damage your carpet or upholstery.

Coming Clean

It's important to remove pet odors from accidents as quickly as possible. Otherwise, your four-legged friends will visit this special little spot over and over again.

If your pets have accidents often, call your veterinarian for advice.

Rust

Treat fresh spots with a solution of 1 cup white vinegar to 2 cups water. If the rust stains dry, have them professionally cleaned.

Tomatoes/Tomato Juice

Sponge the area with cool water and dab with a detergent solution or oxygen cleaner. Rinse with cold water and white vinegar; blot dry.

Wine and Juice

Spritz the area with club soda. Blot and let dry. If the stain remains, repeat the process.

Tar

Use dry-solvent spot cleaner.

Urine, Feces, and Vomit

Ooops! Guess someone shouldn't have had that second ice cream cone and then ridden the upside-down ferris wheel. Apply a detergent solution, oxygen cleaner, or enzyme cleaner. Rinse and blot dry.

Carpet Destroyers
✳ ✳ ✳

Destructive products include acids (toilet bowl and grout cleaners), acne medications, automatic dishwasher detergents, bleaching solutions, drain and oven cleaners, insecticides, pet urine, and plant foods. If you're unsure what to use to clean your carpet, call the manufacturer or store where you purchased it for a recommendation.

Or visit their website(s) for information on how to remove stains.

Visit Your Vacuum

Check the beater brushes regularly and remove threads and hair that wrap around the bar.

To unclog the hose, straighten a wire hanger and slide it in gently to help break up the blockage.

Aid for Allergies

People with allergies may want to consider a vacuum with a HEPA (high-efficiency particulate air) or an ULPA (ultra-low-penetration air) filter to reduce the amount of dust emissions.

When to Call the Carpet Pros
* * *

If you have stains on your carpeting that just won't come out after your best cleaning efforts, it's probably worth it to call in the professional carpet cleaners. But before you do, check out these tips:

Choose a reputable company. Call your local Better Business Bureau or Chamber of Commerce for suggestions. Or ask friends for referrals of carpet cleaning companies.

Check out the prices before you sign anything. For example, stairs are more labor-intensive—some companies charge more for them.

It's smart to look for specials, like "four rooms for only $69," or to use savings coupons. But often companies make the most profit on extras like prespotting and deodorizing.

It's fine to opt for these treatments; just make sure you know the total cost.

Hard Core Floor Care

* * *

Concrete

Scrape and wash the surface properly the first time and you'll have to repaint less often.

After you scrape and wash the floor, apply a commercial concrete etcher; follow all the precautions on the label and wear eye protection. Let it dry 72 hours and then apply paint or stain for concrete floors.

Laminate Materials

Sweep, dust, vacuum, or light damp mop laminates. Avoid wet mopping, which can cause seepage behind baseboards. Never use wax or acrylic products; they can damage the finish.

Use rubbing alcohol to remove nail polish, cigarette burns, shoe polish, paint, ink, or crayon. Use mineral spirits to remove grease or tar.

Love Your Linoleum

Linoleum needs waxing. Use water-based, self-polishing wax. A solvent-based wax can be polished with an electric buffer, but it's a ton of work.

Clean with a commercial cleaner made for linoleum, or a mild detergent and water solution. Rinse with clear water. Don't use ammonia or alkalis. If layers of wax build up (hate that waxy buildup), flooring may discolor.

Use a wax-stripping product for linoleum. Or mix ½ cup to 1 cup ammonia and 1 cup laundry detergent in 1 gallon warm water. Test in an inconspicuous spot to see if it softens the wax film. After several minutes, the area should turn cloudy and soften. Scrub with a stiff brush or electric scrubber. Rinse with clean, cool water. Let dry. (Take a well-deserved nap. Eat chocolate.)

Coming Clean

Tile and Stone Floors

If you want to keep unglazed tile, such as terra-cotta, pristine, vacuum or sweep it frequently—twice daily in a busy family living area.

If you like a natural look, clean less frequently so small particles of dust can help age the surface. (Yeah—love that natural, aged look—on floors only, not my face.)

Sweep and wash with mild detergent or cleaner diluted in water. Lower-rated (and cheaper) tiles are fired at lower temperatures, so the glaze is less durable. Sand and gravel may scratch tiles.

Marble and Granite

Vacuum and damp mop first to remove dirt. Don't wax, polish, or use acidic products— they may etch the stone.

Apply a penetrating sealer before grouting. Treat new quarry tile with linseed oil.

Slate

Vacuum and then mop with a slightly damp mop. Never let water pool on slate—it can damage the surface.

Tile Cleaning Tips
* * *
Too Much Soapy

Remove soap scum with a nonabrasive, all-purpose cleaner or tub-and-tile cleaner. Rinse with water. Buff dry with a clean cloth.

Never use abrasive powders or cleaners containing acids, oils, or organic solvents.

Grout Cleaning Tips

(This grout stuff really makes me grouchy.) Because it's more porous than tile, grout shows stains more— something you might want to consider if you're redoing your bathroom and you're considering tile.

Coming Clean

To clean stained grout, use a strong bleach solution (¾ cup bleach to 1 gallon water) and scrub gently with a small brush. Don't scrub too hard. Wear safety gloves and goggles; keep the entire area well ventilated.

Blood Stains

Dab blood stains with hydrogen peroxide or some diluted bleach.

Coffee, Tea, and Juice

Wash with detergent and hot water; blot with hydrogen peroxide or diluted bleach.

Fat-based Stains

Wash with club soda and water or a nonabrasive floor cleaner. (Or tell your family to stop eating fried chicken in the bathroom.)

Gum, Wax, and Tar

Use an ice bag to solidify the spill. Then gently scrape away as much residue as possible. Remove the residue with some nonflammable paint thinner.

Ink and Dye

Soak a clean cloth with diluted bleach; lay it over the stain. Let it stand until the stain disappears. Rinse well.

Iodine

Scrub with ammonia diluted in water and rinse well.

Nail Polish

Dissolve with nail polish remover. If the stain remains, dab the area with hydrogen peroxide or diluted bleach.

Stamp out Stains on Vinyl Floors
✳ ✳ ✳

Don't use abrasive cleaners, scrubbing tools, or beater-style vacuums. Also avoid harsh detergents, cleansers, and products that give a shiny look. Use only products for no-wax vinyl.

Coming Clean

Black Heel Marks

Rub with an art gum eraser, a nonabrasive scrubbing pad and nonabrasive cleanser, or regular toothpaste. (Better yet, run a shoeless household, making everyone take off their shoes at the door. If they squawk, tell them to pretend they're vacationing in Japan.)

Crayons

(It's a puzzlement how many crayon marks there are everywhere.) Rub the area gently with a cloth slightly dampened with lighter fluid or odorless mineral spirits.

Fruit Juice or Wine

Wash stains with a mild bleach and water solution. If the stains remain, try some rubbing alcohol.

Hair Dye

Use rubbing alcohol. If stains remain, use lighter fluid or odorless mineral spirits. Better yet, only let pros dye your hair. (The last time I did it myself, it looked like a scouring pad come undone.)

Ink

Use rubbing alcohol on ink; then repeat. If the stain remains, use lighter fluid or odorless mineral spirits.

Lipstick

Who's been kissing the floor? Use rubbing alcohol on lipstick.

Paint and Varnish

Wipe up wet spills right away. If the spill has dried, scrape it gently with a plastic card such as a credit card (you won't even get a bill later), or a thin spatula. Remove the residue with rubbing alcohol.

Permanent Marker

Gently rub the mark with lighter fluid, odorless mineral spirits, or rubbing alcohol.

Shoe Polish

Scrub shoe polish with lighter fluid or odorless mineral spirits. If the stain remains, use rubbing alcohol.

Tar

(Where does all the tar come from? We may never know.) Scrub spots with lighter fluid, odorless mineral spirits, or rubbing alcohol.

Be Good to Wood
* * *

To safely wash wood floors, saturate a sponge or rag mop in an oil-soap solution. Wring it almost dry. Damp mop. Rinse with a clean mop dampened in clear water.

For quick dusting, try using disposable electrostatic cloths. For weekly or biweekly cleaning, vacuum with a floor brush attachment on a vacuum cleaner or an electric broom. Don't use a vacuum with a beater bar attachment. It's mean, and it can scratch.

You must neutralize pet stains on wood floors to avoid repeat visits. Use enzymatic cleaners for the best results. To avoid wood damage, dampen the spots and quickly wipe away excess.

Win the Stain Game on Wood Floors
* * *

Dark Spots

Rub with #000 steel wool and floor wax. If the area is still dark, apply bleach or vinegar and allow it to soak into the wood for an hour. Rinse with a damp cloth.

Oil-Based Stains

Rub the area with a soft cloth and dishwashing detergent to break down the grease. Then rinse with clear water. If one application doesn't work, repeat the procedure.

Waxing Wood Floors

* * *

Solid Paste Wax

Use this only for unvarnished hardwood floors, and follow these directions.

Apply the wax by hand for a long-lasting shine. Moisten a soft, lint-free, cotton cloth and wring it almost dry to prevent the cloth from absorbing too much wax. Apply the wax lightly and evenly, working it into the surface.

Wax Not, Work Not

Avoid using excess wax—it attracts dirt. When the floor looks dull, remove old wax finish and rewax, using light coats of wax. Buff the floor with clean toweling.

BYE BYE Wax on Soft-Finish Floors

To remove wax buildup from wood floors without a hard finish, use an all-purpose cleaner and water. After the floor is dry, seal or wax it to protect it.

Hard-Finish Floors

Don't wax these. But if they have already been waxed, you can remove the wax with a commercial wax stripper and a scrubbing pad especially for urethane-finished floors.

Let There Be Light

* * *

Dust ceiling lights and other light fixtures with a feather duster or soft cloth. Turn off the light and wait until the bulb and shade are cool.

To wash, remove the bulbs and glass base. Cover the sockets with some plastic sandwich bags to keep them dry. Wipe the arms and base in warm water and nonsudsing ammonia. Rinse and dry. (Or just invite friends over who are so short that they can't see if your light fixtures are dirty or not. Better yet, choose non-picky friends who'd never think to notice the cleanliness of your lighting.)

Don't touch halogen bulbs with your fingers or cleaning products—it shortens their lives. (And they have only one life to live, after all.)

Cleaning Chandeliers

Be careful with cut-glass or crystal chandeliers. If you use a commercial spray, follow the directions to avoid any damage. Remove the furniture and cover the floors beneath chandeliers.

Woebegone Walls
✳ ✳ ✳

Use semigloss paint for scrubbable finishes in kitchens, baths, children's rooms, and playrooms. If you like flat finishes, choose from light colors—they're less likely to show fingerprints.

Start at the Bottom or Top?

For dusting, start at the ceiling and work down toward the baseboard. Then clean the baseboard and floor. For scrubbing, work from the top to the bottom to move dirt downward and prevent drips.

Vacuum walls with a soft brush attachment and wipe them down with a cloth-covered broom or mop. Spray the walls first with a dusting agent for best results, or use an electrostatic duster.

Wash off fingerprints and other marks immediately. Never scrub plaster or drywall that hasn't been sealed or painted.

Ceramic, Stone, and Brick

Ceramic tile used for bathrooms requires special care because it's prone to soap residue buildup and mildew.

Coming Clean

To remove scum, use a nonabrasive cleaner made for bathrooms, a daily shower cleaner, or white vinegar and water solution. Daily shower cleaners also prevent soap buildup.

Remove crayon marks (oh, those little artists have been busy, haven't they?) from brick or concrete by spraying WD-40 and brushing surfaces with a stiff bristle brush.

Mirrors

Use commercial glass cleaner and soft, lint-free rags to clean mirrors without streaking.

Painted Wall Pointers

Wash latex-painted walls with warm water and a nonabrasive all-purpose cleaner. Dip a clean sponge in the water; then wring dry. Gently rub the wall and rinse again. Wash walls painted with oil-based paint the same way, substituting a detergent solution for the cleaner.

Wallpaper Dirt

Tie a dust cloth or T-shirt sprayed with a dusting agent over your broom to wipe down the walls. Work from the top down. For flocked, grass cloth, or natural-fiber papers, use a soft brush.

Plain, uncoated wallpapers respond best to dry wiping, but can be gently wiped with a damp cloth and then patted dry. Don't let the paper remain wet.

Vinyl Wallpapers

Dust or damp-wipe vinyl wall papers. Vacuum or wipe the wall with a soft rag.

For deep-cleaning, dip a regular sponge in warm water and all-purpose cleaner. Wring almost dry. Lightly scrub the wall in 3-foot sections, rinse with clear water, and pat dry with soft dry cloths.

2

Girls Just Wanna Have Clean

CUT THAT CLUTTER

It's so true. Clutter equals stress. Just say NO!

Now's the time to become the Courageous Clutter

Cutter you've always longed to be. Conquer the

mess fast with these top tips for organizing and

storing everything. All those broken CDs, tattered

toys, outgrown clothes, and appliances with parts

missing are singing "Please Release Me, Let Me

Go." So do it. Do it now. And do it with style—using

unique, thrifty ways of storing the stuff you do

want to keep.

Join the Clutter Cutters' Club

* * *

Have your guests ever stumbled over stuffed dalmatians and unicorns? Do they shriek at the sight of your cat's fake mouse up-ended on the carpet? Or go to get a glass out of your cupboard and get conked on the head with falling objects?

Now that you have the swing of clean from the previous chapter, it's time to declutter.

If clutter is controlling you, make a plan. Set a time to go through your home and all of its contents. (It could be easier when other family members are gone.)

Then systematically get to work, room by room and closet by closet. Allow extra time for such hideous out-of-sight areas as attics, basements, and garages. (And don't feel badly, I had an aunt that used her bedroom as a wastebasket for seven years.)

If your children pile school supplies in the dining room, create study and storage areas in their bedrooms. If your small bedroom closet is packed with clothes, put in those nifty double-hung rods.

As you look at your space, try to incorporate storage as part of your decorating scheme. An étagère (a lovely French word for a freestanding shelving unit) or bookcase can help organize your collections and books.

If space is tight, you can add attractive bins and boxes to the bookcase to neatly conceal personal papers and knitting or sewing projects.

Here's the goal: Clear one room weekly or every two weeks, depending on your time, patience, and mental stability at the moment.

Cut That Clutter

After each room goes from chaos to calm, reward yourself with an inexpensive treat: a BIG candy bar (don't look at the nutrition label or the fat grams), a manicure, or a candlelit bubble bath. Tackle the worst first and you'll feel like a Brave Dirt Warrior.

So have no fear. Mush through the mudroom. Hit high-traffic entryways. Dive through the den. You'll reduce stress fast and find inspiration to get the rest done quickly.

As you work, divide unneeded stuff into one of four boxes: trash, sell, donate, or store someplace else. Many communities have organizations like the Salvation Army or Goodwill that pick these items up at your home.

(Do save at least a few of those ruffled purple, peach, or organza bridesmaid dresses for Halloween costumes or to wear to bridal showers.)

Help–You Need Somebody
* * *
Hire a Pro

If your time is limited and you have the money, play Queen for the Day. Hire help.

A professional organizer can offer advice tailored to you and your family. (And he or she won't tell a soul how messy you are—professional confidentiality applies.)

Areas normally covered are storage planning, managing paper, and busting clutter. Find a professional organizer in your area through the National Association of Professional Organizers at **www.napo.net** on the Web.

Franchised or locally owned closet firms also might offer space planning and storage advice along with installation fees. Be sure to get a written estimate for all services before you sign on.

(If it's going to cost as much as a weekend in Aruba, you might just want to grab your bikini and live with a cluttered closet.)

Just Let It Go

* * *

Hold a Garage Sale

Now is the time for a garage sale. You may even want to go in with your neighbors and have a large sale to share advertising costs and draw bigger crowds.

First, designate a holding area, like some basement shelves. Wash and neatly fold clothing and linens. Keep masking tape and markers or preprinted price stickers handy. Price each item before storing.

On sale day, stay organized. Put similar items together— clothing with clothing, household goods with similar goods—so shoppers can find things easily. Give anything unsold to charity.

Do a Good Deed

Check if the charitable organization will pick up large items, such as furniture. Donated items might be tax-deductible. Be sure and keep a list of your donations and receipts from the organization.

If items are valuable, take snapshots for your records. If you have questions about what and how much is deductible, check with your tax preparer or the Internal Revenue Service. For details on charitable deductions, visit **www.irs.gov**. (They love to have visitors.)

Con$ign for Bucks

If you take items to a consignment shop, they usually pay you 40 to 60 percent of the selling price. (Remember, someone else might just love that tropical shirt with the pink flamingoes your Aunt Bertha sent you for your birthday.)

Take only clothes and furnishings that are clean and in good condition.

Trade-In Options

Look into variations of trade-in policies for such items as infant's and children's clothing that are outgrown long before they wear out.

Buying Bins

Before you load up on storage bins at the discount store, remember that some specialized storage products will become obsolete when your family size or interests change. Before you buy, ask "What else could this hold?"

Hooks and Pegs

These classic solutions were used long before closets. They work well near back doors. And they come in great colors, finishes, and shapes. Flea markets, home furnishings stores, and gift shops sell specialty items, such as old doorknobs mounted on boards, that you can use for storage. Or make your own.

Over-the-Door Organizers

Use these handy products for shoes in a bedroom, toys in a child's room, pantry items in the kitchen, and gift wrap in a crafts room.

Retrofit Containers

For storage, adapt interesting items. Use a work basket or a unique vase for brightly colored, rolled up towels in the bath, or a patterned box for kitchen utensils.

Convert baskets or trunks into coffee tables. Inside, store throws, magazines, newspapers. If space is extremely limited, use trunks or baskets on stands for side tables.

If flea market style is your thing, stack vintage suitcases for side tables. Use interiors to store games, magazines, and seasonal throws.

Flat baskets are good containers for newspapers. (Clear them out daily, or you'll be like my Great-Grandma Minnie, who kept every newspaper since Hitler was defeated for reasons no one ever figured out.)

Magazine racks keep reading material from taking your living area hostage. They come in faux leather, steel, basket weave, etc.

Clear out magazines monthly. Move magazines you want to save to storage units. Just don't get carried away.

Are you really going to ever clip all those low-fat recipes and file them in alphabetical order? (Shame on me, I wouldn't. Although I might save the one for Creamy Chocolate Truffle Torte or all the desserts that include sweetened condensed milk.)

Metal or Plastic Shelving

For long wear and service, look for well-made, smooth, plastic-coated metal shelving or heavy-duty plastic shelving. Typical colors include white, tan, and other neutrals.

Roll-Out Shelving

Available at home centers, it comes in a range of widths and tiers and helps bring items in the back to the front.

Stackable Bins

Sized for newspapers, these also work at the back door for recyclables, such as bottles and cans.

Tiered Metal Plate Racks

Available from home furnishings stores, these are great for potted plants, soaps, towels, or counter storage. You may even find these at garage sales, thrift shops, or dollar stores.

Cut That Clutter

Upright Organizers

These work well for desk or countertop storage. Use them for papers you need to keep for several weeks before filing. Set aside 30 minutes weekly to transfer items, such as bank papers, into your filing system.

Woven Baskets

Baskets provide neat, general storage and transport. Use them for toys or items that need to go to other rooms.

Find More Space
✳ ✳ ✳
Around Windows/Doors

Use the centered wall space above a door for extra display. Build sturdy shelves to show off your heavy collectibles. Use ¾-inch plywood rather than ½-inch and reinforce it with edging strips. This can also work with wide cased openings if you reinforce spans every 24 inches. Better

yet, maybe you can bribe your significant other to build these for you.

Build the top of a window seat with hinges for concealed storage. In a kid's room, sliding front panels may help avoid pinched fingers and getting trapped by an older sibling. (These happenings are always an accident.)

At Your Feet

Build shallow drawers into the toe-kick space beneath base cabinets. Fitted with a touch-latch release, these open with a toe tap.

Banquette Seating

Include built-in seating in compact dining areas. Have seating built with open space underneath, or have doors installed to conceal items. Or build window seats styled with hinged tops to store larger items. (Like the hot dog grilling machine your

Cut That Clutter

hubby got you for your last anniversary that you can't give away without hurting his feelings.)

In the Wall

Carve out shallow display shelves between wall studs. This is ideal for kitchens or baths, where many small items are stored.

Space flanking a fireplace is super for storage. Install bookcases or shelving units.

Fill unfinished space, like dormers, with short stacks of shelves or drawers.

Under the Stairs

This roomy space is often overlooked for storage. Angled and deep, it can be fitted with pull-out, pantry-style shelving units for sporting equipment and games.

(EXTRA BONUS: Then it won't look so dark, spooky, and scary anymore.)

Grinch Every Inch
* * *

In a one-room apartment, or when your living room is also the guest suite, create a sleeping nook. Buy a daybed or futon. Draperies on a ceiling-mounted rod can close for privacy. Buy furniture that serves dual functions. For instance, use a small antique chest for a living room side table.

As an alternative, shop thrift stores for 20th-century reproductions. These are good buys; they look like the originals, but without the high price tags.

If you use a chest to store silver, line it with an antitarnish cloth.

Use trunks wherever you can. For versatility, choose flat tops rather than domes so they can double as tables or benches. Budget wicker trunks are readily available.

Cut That Clutter

Add a low freestanding storage unit or bench to hold books, plants, and favorite accessories under windows. Include 24-inch-deep shelves for oversize books and electronic equipment.

If you live in an apartment or condo with only one outside door, you'll need to be a Brave Clutter Conqueror to keep the entrance clean. Try a narrow console table to collect mail and packages.

Hang a combination mirror/ key rack over it. (That way you won't spend hours looking for your keys, wondering how you could be so forgetful.)

Open shelving is airy, accessible, and economical. Use it to divide space in small living quarters.

Different shelf heights add interest. Use lower shelves for larger volumes. Use upper shelves for standard-size items.

(Just don't get them too high if you're short; dragging a chair over each time to access them gets old fast.)

For dining, use a writing table with a drawer. It can contain everything from flatware and linens to office supplies. Drawer dividers will help keep items handy.

Choose classy versions of kitchen equipment, such as measuring spoons and cutting boards, and put them on countertops as display pieces.

Extend the vanity top over the toilet for maximum shelf space in a tiny bathroom. You can also put hooks (that attach with suction cups) inside the shower area.

Those kitchen or bath storage containers that stick to mirrors or tiles have an urban-chic look that really does the job. You'll find sleek, contemporary ones at most home discount centers.

Winning Entries
✳ ✳ ✳

How does your family use the entryway? Is it a mad pile of unopened bills, dirty mismatched socks, coats, homework, plastic dinosaurs, and toy soldiers missing a few limbs?

Use this space to keep your home running smoothly. Only keep items here that are needed daily, such as car keys and pet leashes.

An umbrella stand is one old-fashioned convenience that serves a practical purpose. Some incorporate stands, or use a tall planter that suits your decor.

It's in the Mail

Envelopes and packages are the usual front-entry cloggers. Control incoming/outgoing mail and small packages with a hall chest.

Use the top drawer for mail. Stow such items as school papers, library books and tapes in drawers. Check drawers daily to avoid fines.

No room for a chest? Place a narrow table or trunk near the front entry.

Take the Back Way

If your family uses a side or back door—and if space allows—use built-ins. Designate cubbies, shelves, or bins for each family member by painting or labeling their names on their very own shelf.

Hang racks, shelves, or pegboards for organizing shopping bags, jackets, and backpacks. Put a smiley face sticker on the cubby that's the neatest each week and a frowny face on the messiest one. (You might get some friendly competition going among your family members.)

Cut That Clutter

A bulletin board or chalkboard is a great place to post activity times and locations. (You can even write fun little notes to each other, like, "Honey, I cleaned the living room," or "Three cheers for Heather—she got an A on her Spanish quiz.")

A bench with storage for boots, gloves, and hats prevents tracking slush inside and dragging soggy coats through the house.

Be a Good Sport

Make one mudroom wall a mini locker with built-ins. Use it for sports gear only.

Measure equipment; rackets, bats, and hockey sticks, and have units built to size. Put small items, such as balls, in bins.

Keep out-of-season gear in the garage or basement, including dirty athletic shoes. Or stuff shoes with newspaper to absorb odors.

Eliminate locker-room aroma by regularly using fabric- and air-sanitizer sprays.

Start at the Top– Attack the Attic

✳ ✳ ✳

An unfinished attic is super for storing items that aren't temperature sensitive, such as holiday decorations and linens, extra sets of dishes, and housewares. Just don't store candles here—they could melt.

(The attic is also a great place to hide out and read a trashy novel and eat chips, if it's not too hot up there.)

Before stashing new items, sort through previously stored boxes and decide if you really need the items. (After all, life has gone on just fine without them so far.)

Store clothes, blankets, and linens for a single season. Clean textiles before storage.

Cut That Clutter

Fabrics need to breathe: Hang them from a garment rack or rod. Keep them dust-free by covering them with a cotton sheet.

Store folded clothing in an acid-free cardboard box or one lined with a clean cotton sheet. Plastic traps moisture, causing mildew.

Or purchase garment bags for long-term clothing storage. If you have lots to store, contact a local moving or storage company. You may be able to buy special boxes with hanging rods from them where you can store your off-season clothing.

If you have insects in your attic, spray baseboards with an all-purpose household insecticide. (It's also fun to buy insect-hotel traps and watch them wander in and never come out.)

No-Nos for Attics
✳ ✳ ✳
Don't Store Books

Mildew and dust are villains, but rodents can be harmful, too, especially if they chew up the ending. (You'll never know if the heiress with amnesia finally gets the million dollars her great-uncle left to her.)

And yes, there is such a thing as a bookworm. Believe me, you don't want to meet one.

Candles and Plastics

Heat will melt these, although you may get some interesting, modernistic shapes.

Formal Clothing

Dust, heat, and attic pests can present problems. Don't risk a wedding or formal dress or valuable heirloom clothing in an attic.

Cut That Clutter

Wedding and christening gowns need professional cleaning and packing. Or store in a climate-controlled area, such as on a shelf of a bedroom closet.

Leather

Changes in temperatures and pests can damage expensive or vintage coats and wraps. If you don't have space, store them at the cleaners.

Photography

Heat destroys slides and negatives, so only put those of ex-husbands or repellent relatives in the attic.

Record Albums

Heat could cause vinyl to warp.

Stuffed Toys

Rodents love toys.

VCR Tapes

Heat and dust can destroy tapes. Although this may be a good storage place for your hubby's copy of "The Dirty Dozen," if you've seen it more than 10 times.

Wood Furniture

Changes in humidity cause wood to expand and contract, resulting in cracks and splits in solid and veneered pieces.

Liven Up the Living Room
* * *
Give It a Great Big KISS

That's KISS, as in Keep It Simple Sister. Your living room should be nice for company, but not so formal you can't relax in it. Arrange it for comfort and easy upkeep. Ditch the excess.

Jazz up a formal living room with built-in bookshelves. Paint the inner back a dramatic color, such as red, to set off collectibles.

Cut That Clutter

Use Trunks and Ottomans

For concealed storage, use trunks or ottomans with hinged lids. Arrange baskets or bins inside for small items.

An accent table and bookrack combination creates chair-side storage with a vintage look.

Vintage tea carts on wheels or reproduction metal utility carts work as temporary bar setups.

Put a television in a cabinet to create a room divider between open living and dining areas. Maximize space by incorporating bench seating with the storage into the room divider. Have the bench crafted so the top lifts for hiding magazines, DVDs or CDs, videocassettes, table linens, or other items.

Use space under a skirted particleboard table to temporarily declutter the room. It's amazing how much stuff you can cram in there—and no one will ever know. Put a console table behind a sofa or against the wall and add squared wicker baskets or trunks with tops. Stack magazines in flat baskets under the table.

Add a shelf around the perimeter of your room for basket storage.

Fun Family Rooms

✳ ✳ ✳

If your kids use the family room for play, a toy box and bins are essential, unless you always want to be tripping over tiny dinosaurs, toy soldiers, and building blocks. Large sturdy baskets are another option.

Even the youngest child soon learns colors and shapes. Purchase bins and boxes in bright colors and tape pictures of items, such as toy cars or doll clothes, on the boxes to avoid confusion.

The position of the television, whether tucked away or open and visible, dictates how much is concealed. Hang a plasma screen television like a painting over a low bookcase filled with bins for tidy storage.

Wardrobes for Storage

Adapt vintage, secondhand, or reproduction wardrobes or armoires as television cabinets. Measure the television, including depth, before you go shopping.

Many vintage pieces are too shallow, but might be usable if a hole is cut in the back for the set to extend out. The back of the unit will have to be drilled or cut for wiring, and shelves will need to be added.

These units are usually large enough to also house the DVD player and CDs or the videocassette recorder and VCR tapes, as well as the cable-TV or satellite hookup box. Include a compact disc player, CDs, and the cassette player and tapes.

Plan built-ins for computer equipment or purchase units geared to your needs. Computer cabinets that resemble armoires are practical in open spaces.

Install floor-to-ceiling metal shelving tracks on one or more walls.

Have ¾-inch thick, 10- to 12-inch-deep plywood planks cut to fit the wall, and hang them from adjustable brackets. Support the shelves at least every 24 inches to prevent sagging. Before anchoring shelves to the wall, check access to electrical outlets and wiring boxes.

Divide shelving into groups of three—an odd number is more visually pleasing. (No one has ever been able to tell me why, but I've tried it myself and it's true.)

Cut That Clutter

Convert a vintage armoire or wardrobe into a liquor cabinet or bar. Reinforce shelves to store heavy bottles. Add a wine rack. Attach under-shelf, track-style hangers designed for footed glasses. Fill flat baskets with corkscrews, stirrers, cocktail napkins, and coasters.

Happy Working from Home

✳ ✳ ✳

Have floor-to-ceiling bookshelves installed. Include shelves around the windows for a library ambience. Or buy stackable storage units or bookcases, often sold in wood finishes.

Hang a painting, print, or photograph from a vertical bookcase support for prominent display. It saves wall space. Stack painted cubes to create shelves. Purchase unfinished bookcases and paint to match.

(It's a definite step up from those brick-and-crate arrangements from dorm-room days.)

Shop home furnishings stores for wall-mounted cabinets or hanging corner cupboards. These are ideal for organizing small objects.

Turn a closet into a library by removing the door, replacing trim, and adding shelves.

Make books and magazines you plan to keep part of the decor by neatly stacking oversize books to serve as small tables. Top with glass, or keep coasters nearby to protect your books. Design, decorating, or travel magazines can look good in similar stacks.

Consider a computer table or storage unit that folds out from a freestanding wardrobe. If you like your armoire, have a cabinetmaker convert it into your own special mini office with sturdy, supported shelves.

Have a cabinetmaker make a vertical pullout storage cabinet for office storage. For efficiency, include plywood organizing dividers and a small bulletin board for notes.

Use pottery, flowerpots, or decorative woven baskets to hold pens, pencils, and scissors. (Don't ever run with the scissors.)

Organize desk drawers with plastic divider trays or boxes to store pens, paper, tape, and stamps. Use file folders to organize papers. Create a color-coded system with bright files (but only if you're really, really bored and just looking for something to do). You can also make your own desk with storage with two contemporary-style filing cabinets to support a glass top. (Make sure glass edges

are beveled for safety.) Use file drawers rather than piling papers on the desk top.

Stack clear or colored bins for dust-free storage.

Use matching metal record bins—available from discount stores—to contain professional journals, other publications, or files.

Conceal less-attractive items (like your husband's giant beer steins or neon bowling trophy) on open shelves inside wicker attaché cases, baskets with tops, well-made picnic baskets, or suitcases.

(Or use that circa 1973 aqua bowling ball as a great garden ornament—a good excuse to get rid of it.)

Office Computer Systems

Protect your computer and software. The biggest enemies of hardware are dust, temperature extremes,

Cut That Clutter

humidity, and smoke. Anything that leads to the contamination or loss of data can be fatal to software.

Never use a magnet to attach notes to the computer. It can erase data. If you must post a reminder, use sticky notes on the monitor frame. (It's better than getting caught mumbling to yourself as you try not to forget.)

Guard against data-scrambling static electricity near hardware by putting plastic mats under your chair and under any machines near the floor; or mist antistatic clothes spray on the carpet once a week.

Give your computer hardware a clean, comfortable environment for a long, healthy life. Put the computer away from heat. Shield it from direct sunlight; this protects equipment. Don't smoke in your computer room. (Ash, smoke, and residue play havoc with keyboards and can get into the central processing unit.)

Unless the computer is a laptop, don't move it. Choose a workstation with room for all your hardware. Don't pack the computer into a small space. The CPU needs room to breathe—at least 2 inches all around.

Store discs in jewelbox cases or in sleeves in sturdy boxes to protect them from dust. One scratch can prevent you from accessing a report.

Dining Rooms That Serve It Up
* * *

Maximize storage with a built-in sideboard or server for china, flatware, and linens. Add a built-in china cabinet with glass doors on both sides to define a dining area without blocking light. Turn an interior wall of your

66

dining room into a sideboard by installing floor-to-ceiling cabinets. Use the top cabinet to store little-used items. If you use some items occasionally, put them somewhere else to free up valuable space for dinnerware you use frequently.

(It'll be a fun surprise when you run across them again—almost like a present.) Use the space between wall studs for shelves to display collectibles.

Fit a compact corner cupboard into a small dining area. Look for vintage pieces or paint an unfinished one.

Use the top for display or plants that require little light. Better yet, get fake plants you can't kill, no matter how much light they get.

No space for a conventional server or sideboard? Buy a small vintage chest. Line drawers with special storage cloth to slow tarnishing if you're storing silver.

A narrow console table also takes up less space than a conventional sideboard when used as a server in a small area.

In an informal dining area, take advantage of the counter between the kitchen and dining room by attaching glass shelves with metal supports. Glass keeps the look open and adds display space.

Combine two metal or wood wine racks with a glass or painted plywood top for a server with storage. Place away from direct sun to avoid damaging the wine.

Make a server table to size by building a plywood frame and having a plywood top cut to fit. Paint the top. Skirt sides using heavy cloth, like tightly woven linen. Staple or hot glue in place.

(A hot-glue gun is a girl's best friend, and it gives you a great sense of power.) Cover staples with fabric cord trim. Use covered space for storage.

Create Your Own Butler's Pantry

✳ ✳ ✳

(No butler is required—more's the pity.) If you have a closet in your dining room, hall, or kitchen, use it.

Buy vinyl stacking bins for dishes (layer with felt to avoid scratches), and hang tracks under shelves for wine glasses. Install cup hooks for cups.

Use flat, lined baskets for flatware. Store sterling silver or silver plate in a specially lined silver chest to avoid tarnish.

Purchase foldout racks used for tea towels to hang linens on the back of the door. Tablecloths, runners, place mats, and napkins will stay unwrinkled. (Hooray, less ironing for you.) You can also construct a butler's pantry by

building shelving around a window in a back hall, or kitchen. Fit stock under-the-counter cabinets with easy-slide drawer glides and wood dividers sized to your china.

Put plastic or wire dividers into drawers, and line them with antitarnish cloth if you store silver there.

Adapt storage to specific needs: Have an upper shelf custom-made for stemware storage, or install stemware tracks (available at hardware stores) under a shelf.

You can also use dowels from a home discount center for vertical plate storage. These are often open on both sides for access.

Use a baker's rack or cupboard to create a handy mini butler's pantry. Shop for a baker's rack with wide lower shelves for a convenient serving counter.

Kitchen Storage

* * *

Add style with interesting items. Use a new or vintage fish poacher to organize oils and condiments. Or store spices in test tubes.

Store rarely used items in large bowls or crocks along cabinet tops. Collect pitchers, painted pails, and crocks to hold serving utensils. Buy a wooden expandable rack with pegs to hang mugs. (This makes them easy to grab before that much-needed first jolt of java.)

Keep envelopes of soup or salad dressing mix in berry baskets.

Organize shelves with revolving racks for spices and staples. (They're fun to spin too.)

Coping with Cabinets

Let's get real. Even if your idea of cooking is removing the box before zapping a frozen dinner in the microwave, there's never enough kitchen storage space.

Standard cabinets are widely available, but custom-made cabinets with both deep and shallow drawers might better organize items.

Fit the inside of cabinet doors with racks to easily find cookware lids and canned goods. For ultimate accessible storage, use open wall storage and open under-the-counter storage instead of conventional closed cabinets.

Be selective when storage space is tight. As you buy cookware, collect types that display well together.

Store rice, beans, flour, cornmeal, cereal, and dry staples in sealed see-through containers. You'll keep pests away and know supply levels.

Also use containers for small packets of sauce mixes. (But

Cut That Clutter

chances are, those fast-food restaurant hot sauce packets from three years ago can go bye-bye.)

Use Square Containers

Square containers are more space-efficient than round ones. (Don't loan out your storage containers. People mean well, but you rarely get them back, and if you do, they can be stained.)

Platters and bowls fit well in drawers with dividers. Check with a cabinet firm or home improvement center for ideas.

Maximize work space by keeping appliances that you use every day on the counter. Hang utensils from wall-mounted pegboards.

Install a counter-to-ceiling grid on a blank wall. Hang cookware and utensils from S hooks. Scout architectural salvage shops for interesting ironware.

Mount a narrow shelf on the backsplash to keep salt, pepper and mugs off of the countertop.

Note: Such storage is convenient for herbs and spices, but these keep better stored away from heat. Use space-saving tiered spice "steps" on a counter or in a cabinet.

Hang glass shelves across a window. They let in light and can show off colorful bottles.

Purchase a hanging cabinet or corner cupboard for open storage. If a vintage piece has a timeworn finish, enjoy the patina.

Buy ready-made picture ledges, available from decorating shops, and have a frame shop rout grooves for plates (or do it yourself). Hang them as plate racks to display dishes.

Cut That Clutter

Island Option

(Sorry, this is about work space, not a trip to Waikiki.)

Buy a butcher-block cart on wheels from a specialty home-design catalog or kitchen shop. Look for one with storage, such as a wine rack.

If you don't have a pantry, add shelves to the back of the kitchen door to store canned goods and seasonal items.

Use a hook-over-the-door organizer with shoe pockets for packets of dry goods, such as soup or gravy.

Try using large decorative jars to hold bulk quantities of foods. Before buying jars for this purpose, ask whether the finishes are safe for food. (Don't buy in bulk if you're single—it could take you decades to eat all of this.)

Use acrylic or natural-woven baskets with compartments to store flatware and napkins. Use a chrome-plated steel basket with handles to keep fresh fruit neatly arranged, or store kitchen towels in it.

Remember to Recycle

A standard base cabinet is normally sized to hold two kitchen bins—easy to divide glass from plastic. Pullout shelves make access easy. If your kitchen is above a walk-out basement or garage, cut a chute in a base cabinet that leads directly to separate receptacles on the lower level. Or set bins on plastic shelving outside the back door.

What to Recycle
✳ ✳ ✳

Contact your local collection service for what's recyclable in your area.

Glass

Rinse food jars to avoid attracting insects. Beverage bottles might be refundable.

Cut That Clutter

Get your kids to return them and let them keep the money for a special treat. It will save you a trip and make them feel good for helping.

Newsprint

Stack these in boxes or bins you already have. In some areas, newspapers must be tied with twine.

Metal Cans

Rinse to avoid pests. To save space, remove lids and flatten cans by stepping on them.

Because of their sharp edges, metal lids often are banned from recycling. (TIP: Rinse lids and collect them in an empty, round oatmeal box that can be tossed when full.)

Drink Cans

Beer and soft-drink cans are often returnable for a deposit at grocers or recycling centers. Some cities require you to sort cans from paper.

Boxes

Flattening might be required. If recycling isn't an option, community groups often need sturdy, clean ones. Please don't stuff the garage with them or you'll be sorry later when you're looking for more storage space.

Plastics

Some bottles are refundable. Rinse well, as sugars attract pests and sour milk smells really bad, especially on hot days.

Kitchen Clutter Disaster Quiz

✳ ✳ ✳

Scrambling each morning to find the whisk for the eggs? Need a construction crane to dig out the roasting pan? There are ways to correct these problems and create a functional kitchen. Take this quick quiz to see if you could use some help. (I know I did.)

Cut That Clutter

1. Do you have to move more than one baking dish to reach the one you need?
2. When storing leftovers, do you have to search to find the proper size bowl and/or matching lid?
3. Do you even have lids for your storage containers?
4. Does it take more than 10 seconds to grab the right pan lid or the turkey baster or the hand mixer?
5. Have you ever tripped over the kitchen trash can?
6. Have you ever said a naughty word when you did that?
7. Do you have a full set of wine glasses, or do late-arriving guests have to use assorted coffee mugs?
8. Do you have to get on your hands and knees and dig around in cabinets to get the right size pot or pan?
9. Do you keep your electric hair rollers on your kitchen counter?
10. When baking, do you gather utensils from all over the kitchen?
11. Do you have more than one "junk" drawer?
12. Do your kids complain that your chips are always stale because you don't have those handy-dandy bag clips?

If you answered yes to any of these questions, there's still hope! Consider these space- and time-saving strategies. (The stuff to make these changes is readily available at hardware and home improvement stores.)

- Consider installing tambour-door appliance garages (the same type of system as on a roll-top desk) between your base and wall cabinets to store gadgets out of sight, yet within reach.

- To make it easier to reach items stored at the back of base cabinets, replace the fixed shelves with pullout trays. Use baskets to organize similar items,

Cut That Clutter

keeping them together for quick and easy access.

- Install vertical partitions in cabinets to store pan or storage container lids, trays, cookie sheets, and baking dishes vertically.

- Customize "junk" drawer(s) with cutlery trays.

- Install lid holders on the inside of cabinet doors for lightweight items.

- Stemware racks and cup hooks improve access to glassware, cups, and mugs, and make the most of upper-cabinet storage.

- Install a pullout trash basket in a base cabinet. Is the garage off the kitchen? Consider using a small magnetic swinging flap to toss items through and into the can in the garage. (In some areas, building codes require a security lock on any access into the home. And keep an eye on the dog or cat that might confuse it with a pet door.)

- If you like the look, hang pots from a ceiling rack.

- Store spices in wire racks attached to the interior doors.

- Shelves that hug the walls of the broom closet need only be 3½ inches deep to provide additional storage for cleaning supplies or canned goods.

- Store items you use together near each other. Save steps by duplicating items frequently used elsewhere as well.

- Install a pot rack to keep pans convenient and free up cabinets.

- Don't overdo it with cutesy refrigerator magnets. It can result in a cluttered look.

Beautiful Bedrooms
✳ ✳ ✳

Use the space under the bed for heavy-duty plastic or cardboard storage boxes. (Purchase boxes with tight-fitting lids to keep out the dust.)

These containers work well for out-of-season items. Use them for belongings you don't need daily but that require climate control, such as photographs.

Buy a bed with integral, under-the-mattress storage. Check with a full-service furniture store.

Choose perforated clothes hampers. (The perforations will ensure that you don't faint when you open the lid and encounter your kids' dirty soccer clothes.)

Even more convenient: Buy two hampers. Use one for washable clothing and one for items for the dry cleaners.

In a country- or cottage-style bedroom, use white wicker hampers. Shop antique stores or flea markets for unique vintage hampers.

In a bedroom with little storage, use decorative cubes with lift-off lids. These work well for matching bedside tables or at the foot of the bed. Specialty home decorating stores carry variations of the handy, versatile storage wood cube.

Get double duty from nightstands by placing a decorative box from an import store on a stand. Such hinged boxes work well as lamp tables and are easy to access and handy for tissues, glasses, reading material, and miscellaneous necessities.

When you need maximum storage for items such as hats and bulky quilts, add a vintage trunk or chest at the foot of the bed. Affordable wicker is easy to move.

Cut That Clutter

Skirt a particleboard table and use the space underneath for stacked boxes. Some plywood table bases are made with a shelf for stacked boxes.

Add a padded or wooden bench and use the space underneath to stash out-of-season items in wicker suitcases or other decorative boxes. Take advantage of bedroom walls with floor-to-ceiling shelving.

Store That Jazz

Use the space on your dresser or chest to jazz up your bedroom. Stack clear boxes to keep earrings, costume jewelry, socks, tights, hose, or scarves handy.

All that glitters dresses up the dresser. (And remember, nothing succeeds like excess when it comes to glitter.) Create affordable dresser-top storage with serving trays from an import store.

Purchase honeycomb-style drawer dividers. Most dividers expand to fit drawers and are easily installed. They're great for small accessories.

Another thrifty tip: Buy plastic ice cube trays, spray-paint them in fun colors, and use them to store pairs of earrings.

Heights for Closet Rods

Double rods: 82 and 42 inches
Single rod: 72 inches
Long dresses: 69 inches
Robes: 52 inches
Dresses: 45 inches
Pants (cuff hung): 44 inches
Men's suits: 38 inches
Skirts: 35 inches
Women's suits: 29 inches
Blouses or shirts: 28 inches
Pants (folded over): 20 inches

Create the type of storage configurations you need with easy-to-attach stock wood or wire shelves. Components are sold at discount stores and home centers.

Cut That Clutter

Take advantage of the variety of styles. Ready-made, vinyl-coated shelving units are sturdy and economical.

You can easily attach racks or shelves to closet walls or doors. Or, if you have the space, you can try freestanding units.

Group clothes by purpose. Keep business and dress clothes together, casual together, and crossover ones in the middle. Arrange them by color and style.

Use wooden or padded hangers. ("No more wire hangers!" as Faye Dunaway so unforgettably put it in the movie "Mommy Dearest.") Pants hangers hold sharp, pressed creases, but avoid wrinkles from folding.

Use shoe racks, shelves, and hanging bags. Shoe trees help leather shoes and boots keep their shape.

Line up shoes by purpose and color, and keep slippers and sneakers handy. (And remember, a girl can never have too many shoes.)

Utilize space under hanging shirts or blouses with a low chest or wicker hamper for out-of-season clothes. Add a shelf above the rod to use wasted space for your out-of-season items.

Use boxes to protect hats from dust. Group purses and totes by size and season.

Pegs, hooks, or racks on the insides of closet doors hold hats, ties, scarves, and belts. Use hooks only for heavy robes or belts.

(Clothing doesn't hang well on hooks. It may develop odd creases and lumps that make you look like you're giving a free ride to a small gerbil underneath your jacket.)

Cut That Clutter

Remove clothes from dry cleaning bags. Humidity inside bags can cause yellowing. Cedar blocks next to your clothes can too.

Let clothing air before hanging it to let body moisture escape. Clothes stay clean and last longer.

If clothes are spilling out of your closet, buy a freestanding clothes rack and angle it in a corner of the room behind a screen.

(Or, if you have an extra bedroom, do what one of my friends did and turn it into a closet with freestanding racks.)

Rockin' Kids' Rooms

✳ ✳ ✳

Center the crib in the room and add matching storage units on either side. In a tiny nursery, borrow space from a closet by removing doors. Add a small baker's rack for easily accessible storage.

When space is tight, purchase a small corner cupboard for extra storage. (Bolt it to the wall so it can't tip over.)

Purchase a crib or changing table with integral storage underneath. Stretch your budget by buying a secondhand chest or dresser and painting it a bright color.

Install Shaker pegs or hooks near the door:

1. Cut a 1×3-inch pine board to length.
2. Using wood glue, fasten board to the wall.
3. Cut two pieces of ½-inch-wide decorative molding the same length; nail flush to the top and bottom of the board with nails.
4. Drill holes for 3-inch-long Shaker pegs 5 inches apart; glue pegs in holes.

Cut That Clutter

Buy a child-size coatrack. Install an expandable rack with pegs for jackets, caps, and mittens, or to display special dress up outfits.

Drop a closet rod to a height children can reach; use upper rods for out-of-season clothing. Use hanging closet organizers, such as shoe or sweater bags, to keep clothing at eye level. Install a few decorative hooks nearby for hanging robes.

Work with a cabinetmaker to build a twin-size platform bed with drawers underneath. Pullout drawers are safer than toy boxes.

Drawers work well for older kids' extra bedding, sports equipment, projects, and their collections.

Purchase a bed designed with storage (many times it's underneath). Check with stores that handle youth furniture for prices.

Consider modular furniture for a built-in look that's movable. Pair storage pieces with a desk along a wall or in a closet. Incorporate a trunk on casters for clothes storage and a bedside table.

Place the bed against the back of a freestanding wardrobe, making a walk-in dressing area behind the bed. If the piece has an unfinished back, staple or glue fabric to cover rough edges.

Build removable shelves in one end of the closet. Store children's everyday toys and games on low shelves that they can reach.

Build a low corner bookcase with smooth edges for safe storage. Measure what you plan to store before installing the shelves. Make shelving adaptable for changing needs, and weight loads. (I think I know what accounts for mine: pasta, chocolate, and really good bread.)

Cut That Clutter

Architects often specify ¾-inch-thick birch plywood for bookshelves; spans should be no more than 30 to 36 inches between supports.

If using thinner plywood, such as ½-inch, place supports every 24 inches. Economical particleboard, rather than laminate, works fine for built-ins. Paint the completed unit to suit your decor.

Acquire storage pieces that can be used through teen years. A dresser and armoire ideal for baby clothes and diapers works equally well for jeans and T-shirts.

Add clear plastic bins in children's closets to organize toys without concealing them. You might want to buy them in your kids' favorite colors, to encourage them to use them.

Paint a chest with blocks of color for coded organizing.

Building sets, games, crayons, puzzles, and assorted small items can drive parents crazy. Keep them out of the toy box, where they're lost forever. Use drawer organizers or cleaning caddies and store on shelves. (That way you don't have to listen to: "I can't find little pink pony's purple tie-on mane," or "Where's my stuffed toy bear's collar?")

For children in upper elementary or middle school, look for chests to paint and use for storage. Add plastic drawer dividers or stackable storage bins so items don't get lost in a deep chest.

Purchase plastic crates for a room divider with storage. Link two rows of crates for a divider that has access from both sides.

As soon as your kids have homework, provide desks with storage. As a budget-stretcher, shop for vintage or unfinished desks to paint.

Cut That Clutter

Standard desks are 30 inches high; computer stands are 26 inches high.

You can also make a desk. Create two stacks of plastic crates. Lash the crates together. Space stacks to allow knee space between. Lay a plywood top with rounded corners, sanded smooth and painted, across the pair.

Make a study desk from painted metal or wood filing cabinets. Paint or stain a 4-foot-long, 1-inch-thick wood plank or door that fits the cabinets' depth.

Hostess with the Mostest
* * *

Turn a home office, den, or family room into a guest room with a fold-down bed unit, a.k.a., a Murphy bed. Order these modular units with open shelving that doubles as side tables for guests, plus a desk and files. Units also work well installed between bookcases.

Remember that guests show up with suitcases and need a place to put things. (Hopefully not your Aunt Ida on an unannounced visit, planning to stay three weeks with Fifi Louise, her elderly shih tzu.)

Install a bank of built-in closets across a room wall. Put in shoe shelves. Store items such as luggage under the bed. Hang fabric panels on wire line or a drapery rod suspended from the ceiling to conceal storage (or any family members who are acting rather peculiar at the moment).

Visitors need things to do without always being with you. (Good ways to entertain them: Have them organize your cupboards or clean your attic. Just kidding.)

Purchase matching bookshelf units for a reading nook. Paint or stain them to match your decor. Set a TV on top for entertainment.

Add storage to a traditional-style bedroom. Shaker, wicker, or wooden boxes enhance the look while hiding necessities.

Use an antique steamer trunk for storing blankets or out-of-season clothing. Be creative with specialized storage. Add wooden, woven, or art-paper-clad boxes to store papers, magazines, or mending.

Cover a plain cardboard box and its removable top with heavy gift paper, brown kraft paper, or colorful wallpaper scraps for affordable, attractive storage.

(If you have leftover scraps, you can use them for colorful all-occasion gift wrapping.)

Specialty Closets
* * *
Cedar Closets

Cedar closets can help protect your clothing and textiles from insects and mildew. The cedar closet or chest must have a tight fit. Freshly launder clothing and textiles before storing them.

To make a cedar closet effective, eliminate airflow under the door and through electrical outlet covers, open screw holes, or holes made by hooks. Cedar chests are often a good choice because they are fitted with tight sides and heavy lids.

You can also line a closet with cedar over existing drywall or studs. Use ¼-inch tongue-and-groove boards or 4×8 panels featuring a cover of cedar chips. Panels are easy to install, budget-priced, and are fragrant. Deck cedar doesn't have the same properties.

Cut That Clutter

Maintain the Aroma

Leave the cedar panels or boards unfinished to enjoy the scent. If the cedar loses its fragrance or its surface becomes hard, sand lightly to restore.

(Take a deep sniff and pretend you're doing aromatherapy at an expensive spa.)

But, remember, cedar blocks and chips do not prevent moth larva damage. (Chomp. Chomp.)

Linen Closets
✳ ✳ ✳

Separate bed linens by size, style, or sheet sets. Tie sets together with ribbon or encase in a matching pillow cover.

Rotate sheets for even wear by putting freshly washed linens at the bottom of the stack and using sheets from the top.

Organize towels by type (bath, hand, fingertip) or by color for easy identification. Group table linens by type, such as tablecloths and runners.

Install door racks for convenient storage, or hang items on quality wooden or plastic hangers.

Store napkins by the set. If the linen closet isn't convenient, put napkins in a sideboard or chest of drawers close to the dining room.

When fine linens include matching place mats and napkins, sandwich each pressed set between cardboard.

Use baskets, bins, or plastic-coated wire shelving. When space allows, store extra or out-of-season comforters or blankets on separate shelves. Add fragrant sachets. If you use your linen closet to store toiletries, use storage bins to organize items together.

Baths
* * *
With an Ahhhh Feeling

For a fresh start, clear the decks. (Get rid of that calamine lotion you bought after your camping trip three years ago. Ditch that purple zinc oxide you were going to use on a cruise to the Bahamas.)

Add a shelf with brackets over the tub. If storage needs are great, put a shelf over the door.

For extra storage when the toiletry cabinet is overflowing, install a clear acrylic shelf on brackets above the sink. Use plastic canisters or small pieces of pottery to hold small items.

Replace a small mirror-front medicine cabinet with one that spans the width of the counter. Choose one that has shelf space behind the entire mirror. Add small baskets to organize such items as nail clippers.

Hang a hook on the back of the door too. Or a door-hinge towel rack also works well and doubles as a clothing hook.

Metal hooks, in a variety of styles and finishes, give a sleek, updated look. Heated towel bars are an affordable luxury. Find them at home centers, bath-and-linen stores, and discount stores.

Add a storage basket, wicker hamper, or stackable containers underneath the skirt for storage. If you have kids or pets, don't store cleaners or medicines under the sink, where they can get into them.

Convert a chest or small sideboard into a vanity and have a marble or granite top cut to fit. Or start with a self-rimming sink.

Cut That Clutter

Clear the countertops by using wall-mounted hooks or pegs topped with shelving for blow dryers or curling irons.

In a powder room, use a large decorative bowl for guest towels. Metal or wicker baskets also work well. Use a vintage dish or a small tiered plate rack to hold guest soaps.

Turn a metal basket, such as a vintage egg basket, into a decorative container for rolled towels or extra toilet tissue.

Use containers that attach to nonporous surfaces with suction cups for razors or bath poufs.

Basement Basics
* * *

With precautions, an unfinished basement without ventilation, heating, and cooling can be used for items that are unaffected by moisture. Basements are good storage for extra dishes, pottery, and tools.

Basement Blues

(It isn't only in horror films that it's best to stay upstairs.) Many household items suffer if stored down there, especially if it's dank and dark. (But however bad your basement is, don't be ashamed. Last time I moved, I filled three dumpsters with basement clutter and considered joining Basement Bums Anonymous.)

Don't Put These in Your Basement!
* * *
Books

Moisture and mildew may damage pages and expensive, leather-bound volumes.

Heirloom Clothing

Basement moisture and mildew are the worst offenders to clothing.

Cut That Clutter

Photography

Moisture, mildew, and temperature changes harm photos and negatives. Order your pictures on CDs and toss the negatives. (Kind of like you toss out any negative, unsolicited feedback from your relatives.)

Outer Space
* * *
Garage and Shed

Install a pegboard or vinyl-coated metal grid system with hooks for small items and hand tools. Group by function. Install heavy-duty hooks for large shovels and rakes.

Look up for overhead space. Tubular steel hooks can hang tools, sporting goods, ladders, lumber, and lawn furniture. Check out home centers and storage stores for workbenches that expand.

Lofty Heights

If space allows, use a loft in the garage for overhead space. It's ideal for sports gear, luggage, and holiday ornaments. Include a locked metal chest or cabinet for dangerous tools and pesticides.

Mount bicycles on the wall. Bicycle shops and home centers have racks for keeping bikes flush to the wall. (It's better for the tires too). Add an accessory rack for helmets and equipment.

Out in the Open

If you have an open carport and space allows, use it for storage by adding a locked closet that keeps tools or sports gear handy and out of sight. Weather-resistant plastic cabinets work well, too, and can be padlocked. Secure tools with bike locks.

If you must store tools in an open carport, screw a heavy-duty U-bolt into a support post.

Secure tools by looping a bike lock chain through the handle and the U-bolt, and lock it up.

Take advantage of the space under the deck if it's at least 4 feet off the ground. Use this for items usually exposed to the weather, such as the barbecue grill or outdoor toys.

Screen underdeck storage with a lattice to keep out wildlife. (Evicting a skunk is no fun. But, if you do get sprayed, tomato juice will remove the aroma. I just know it works, I don't know why.)

Install adjustable shelving against a wall. Use see-through plastic bins to store small items.

Store fertilizers, bulb boosters, deicing chemicals, and other hazardous items on top shelves in plastic bins. Keep away from kids and pets.

Plan Outdoor Storage Safety
✳ ✳ ✳

A garden shed at the back of your yard (but away from the neighbor's garage) often is the safest place for flammable substances. When you bring home new fuels, oils, and paints, see if they're flammable or have special storage requirements. If so, keep them away from kids and pets and store outside your home. Never store them near the water heater or clothes dryer.

Charcoal Lighter Fluid

Store away from children on a high shelf or in a locked cabinet. Keep away from heat. (This stuff is scary.)

Gas Grills

Disconnect the propane cylinder from the grill, shut off the valve, and put the plug in the valve.

Propane gas is volatile, and leaks are slow. Store outside in a protected area inaccessible to kids. A well-ventilated toolshed is a good choice.

Lawn Mowers

If gas-powered, drain gas at the season's end. For a combination of gas and oil, drain fuel into a container, mark it clearly, and arrange for hazardous waste disposal. Keep it away from kids.

Paint and Solvents

Seal cans tightly and turn them upside down. The paint will seal against oxygen and stay fresh longer. Keep latex paints from freezing.

Vapors from solvents are a fire hazard. Store them in upright sealed containers in a well-ventilated place.

Pesticides

Buy just enough for the season. For organic alternatives that avoid storage problems, check gardening books and your county extension service. Keep away from kids.

Protect Your Papers
* * *
Set Up a System

Maintaining complete and accessible records—short term and long term—is an important part of making your home run smoothly. (The IRS gets cranky when you can't find your tax returns.)

If you have a loan coupon book, keep it and addressed, stamped envelopes together. After you open the mail, file things promptly. Start with bills. Open everything immediately and check the due date.

File coupons you clip by expiration date. (But be sure to use them or The Coupon Police will come after you. I don't think there are Coupon

Cut That Clutter

Police. They would have found me by now.) When ordering entertainment or travel tickets in advance, file them in envelopes in a logical place; replacements can be difficult and costly.

Save appliance manuals and warranty information in one place, such as an oversized binder with pocket sleeves.

Keep computer manuals by the computer. Record serial and model numbers on each; attach the original bill. Store master software disks and registration numbers near your computer. You'll need the registration number for technical support.

Records to Keep

- Account numbers
- Bonds, securities, and stock certificates
- Social Security cards
- Passports
- Birth certificates
- Loan papers, contracts
- Mortgage papers/lease

- Abstracts and deeds
- Adoption, marriage, and divorce papers
- Safe-deposit box key and inventory of contents (keep at home)
- Insurance policies
- Inventory (list and videotapes or photographs of household possessions)
- Wills

You likely don't need to save:
- Lists of men you dated
- Notes about every kind of shoe you've owned in your lifetime
- A record of how many times you asked your hubby or significant other, "Honey, does this make my rear end look fat?" By the way, here are the correct answers to that question:
    1. Of course not!
    2. No way!
    3. What rear end?

Review your personal property insurance coverage annually. Actual cash value subtracts depreciation from the cost of replacing a damaged item.

Cut That Clutter

If you own big-ticket items, consider adding riders to cover these, such as expensive musical instruments, jewelry, and artwork.

Records to Shred

Identity theft is no joke—it's the fastest increasing crime. Don't let anyone steal Social Security, bank account, or credit card numbers.

Such numbers will be on payment statements, copies of credit card slips, and numerous other financial, purchasing, and personal records. Often, they're on various solicitations you get in the mail.

To be safe, get a desktop shredder. They're available at office supply and discount stores for a reasonable price.

Secure Protection
* * *
Provide secure protection for your records—especially ones that don't exist elsewhere. At home, use a waterproof, fire-resistant lockbox.

Waterproof containers are double-walled and insulated. Fire protection for up to one hour at 1,700 degrees F is best; paper chars at 350 degrees F. Put the key in a secure spot.

For off-site secure storage, consider the safe-deposit box service at your bank. Bank lobby hours determine when you can get to your box.

Special Storage
* * *
CDs

Dusty or scratched discs don't play. If you own a CD burner, copy your CDs and keep the originals for copies to replace in case of loss or scratching.

Cut That Clutter

Family Photographs

Humidity, fingerprints, light, and dust damage photos; handle prints by edges only. Keep photos in dry places.

(On the envelope, mark the important dates and subjects, such as your Dad at a roadside Wall Drug sign in 1977 or your little brother trying to climb The World's Largest Ball of Twine.)

Reprinting from negatives results in better quality than copying photos, so keep negatives safe. Never touch them or cut them apart.

Indicate which set of pictures came from the negatives. Keep envelopes in a dust-resistant case or import negatives to your computer hard drive for digital storage.

If you use slides instead of prints, remember they are originals. No negatives exist.

(If only life could be that way too.) Protect slides by storing them in acid-free or metal, baked-enamel-finish boxes or in polypropylene slide pages.

Leaving slides in projector carousels subjects them to moisture, which causes warping and dust collection. Keep all photographic images out of the direct sunlight.

Keepsakes

These are often delicate (like the dried-up remains of your Primrose Prom corsage, or the giant panda from the 1969 State Fair)— of value to you, but perhaps no one else.

But guess what? Since you're the one who's organizing, you get to keep what YOU want. Keep what you can't part with in a hope chest, and store it in a cool, dry area so the items won't be affected by mold or mildew.

Girls Just Wanna Have Clean

3

FABULOUS FURNISHINGS

Your rooms and accessories reflect your personality, your adventures, your loves, your life. Whether it's those window treatments you created with floating pastel strips of chiffon, the magenta maracas from Mexico, or your collection of '50s salt-and-pepper shakers, you'll maintain them in prime condition with the expert tips and advice in this chapter. And we'll have a little fun along the way too.

Fabulous Furnishings

Let's Talk Tools

✳ ✳ ✳

You Get to Shop Again!

Here's what you'll need:

Art Gum Eraser

Soft and pliable, it's safe for cleaning delicate surfaces. (You can even pretend you're a famous artist as you clean.)

Brooms and Brushes

Have a clothing brush (bristles on one side, velvety nap on the other), soft paint brush, suede brush, utility brush, whisk broom, floor broom, and a toilet brush. (I'm so glad these toilet brushes now come in collectors' colors, with a tidy little caddy to tuck them in.)

Classic Feather Duster

A true ostrich-feather duster removes dust from delicate surfaces. Don't get inexpensive synthetic ones—they might scratch surfaces.

Duster for Blinds

Soft-fiber fingers slide between blinds.

Electrostatic Dusters

These include the colorful fluffy-hairy heads on various-length wands, as well as disposable sheets that attach to floor-cleaning or furniture-cleaning handles.

Lamb's Wool Duster

One with a long wand is ideal for hard-to-reach areas, such as light fixtures and ceiling fans. The lanolin-rich fibers attract dirt.

Lint Roller

These sticky rollers trap kitty and doggy hair as well as lint.

Mops

Use sponge mops, mops with washable terry cloth covers, or a floor-cleaning system with a battery-operated cleanser dispenser and

Fabulous Furnishings

disposable pads. (WARNING: This last choice is very heavy and you'll likely need help carrying it into your home, unless you've recently trained for the World Cup Triathlon.)

Squeegee

A quality rubber squeegee makes cleaning windows and showers easy. (And it's such a fun word to say: squeegee, squeegee, squeegee. Love it.)

Treated Cloths

Soft, treated cloths hold dirt. Use them in place of silicon sprays on fine wood.

Vacuum Attachments

These usually include a soft upholstery brush, blind-cleaning attachment, and crevice tool.

White Cotton Cloths and Cheesecloth

Use these to blot, clean, and polish.

Fine Furniture Care
* * *

Bamboo

Wipe these with a slightly damp, soft cloth. Be gentle with older bamboo pieces. (In general, be gentle with anything or anyone old. They've existed a long time, and you may learn something important from them.)

Cane

Wipe with a soft, dry cloth. Inspect for damage. Tack loose corners. Have a furniture restorer repair tears.

Chrome

Spray glass cleaner on a soft cloth and rub gently. Check for rust spots. Treat with polish for chrome.

Gilded Finishes

Papier-mâché tables found at thrift stores or flea markets may have gilded finishes. Dust with a feather duster

Fabulous Furnishings

or a soft paintbrush. Never use water to clean gilded pieces. Use a soft cloth dipped in odorless paint thinner that's been warmed by putting the sealed bottle in a bucket of warm water. Gently pat gilded areas; don't rub, especially on the gilded areas, if they're flaking.

Leave restoration to the professionals. Don't attempt to touch up with gold tone paint; it won't match.

(Also don't try to patch chips or nicks with gold tone nail polish from the drugstore as I once did—disaster!)

Glass

Use commercial glass cleaner or mix 2 tablespoons vinegar in a quart of water. Moisten cloths and wipe glass surfaces. Rinse with clear water and wipe with a dry cloth.

For sticky spots, dip a cloth in a water-and-vinegar solution. Lay it on the spot

until the residue dissolves. Paint, glue, and household products that can't be dissolved with vinegar or commercial cleaners can be scraped with a razor blade. Avoid scratches; don't slide objects on glass. And be CAREFUL.

Inlays

Check that pieces are tightly adhered to the frame. Unless you're sure the pieces are tight or have a durable seal, don't vacuum. (Hooray for you—one less thing you have to vacuum.)

Use a feather duster instead of a cloth that might catch small edges and chip patterns.

Materials other than wood—including mother-of-pearl or ivory—may be inlaid. Clean with a mild detergent and water. Wring the cloth almost dry and wipe the surface. Dry immediately with a second lint-free cloth. Seal with clear paste wax.

Fabulous Furnishings

Laminates

Wash these surfaces with warm water and mild detergent. Rinse thoroughly. Dry immediately. Don't use abrasive cleaners or pads, as they could scratch.

Check for loosening laminate. If it starts to loosen, work wood glue or laminate glue between the laminate and the wood base. Wipe off any excess. Place a soft cloth over the laminate and, if possible, clamp it until the glue dries.

Leather

Small, shallow scratches often add character and blend in over time. Use leather dye for deep scratches.

Manufacturers may sell touch-up kits to help repair scratches or nicks on furniture. Consider buying one when you purchase the piece, in case the color is discontinued. If you have several leather pieces, label the kits to avoid confusion.

Aged Metals

Reproduction pieces may continue to rust or leave powdery rust flakes. Wipe the metal gently with tack cloths (they have a slightly sticky surface to help pick up dust particles).

Wire-brush any rough spots. Seal with matte-finish polyurethane. Or, prime and spray-paint with products formulated for metals.

New Metals

Dust wrought iron, steel, and aluminum with soft cloths. Clean them with a solution of 2 tablespoons vinegar to 1 cup water. Rinse with clear water and dry. Put furniture protectors under legs to avoid rust spots on carpet or scratches on wood or tile. (See Chapter 1 for tips on how to choose a floor protector.)

New Paint

Wipe the surface with a clean, slightly damp cloth dipped into warm water mixed with either all-purpose cleaner or vinegar. Rinse.

For stubborn soiling, make a paste of baking soda and water, rubbing in the paste with a nonabrasive pad. Or dampen a cloth with rubbing alcohol and wipe the wood.

Rinse with clear water. Dry immediately.

Clean decoratively painted and sealed new furniture like you would plain painted pieces. For unsealed decorated furniture, use vinegar diluted in warm water.

Old Paint

Unless the piece has a delicate painted finish, use a whisk broom to clean it with the grain. Vacuum with a soft brush attachment. Don't scrub loose paint.

Determine whether paint on old furniture contains lead before removing it. Test kits are available at most hardware stores. It may be safer to seal the paint with matte-finish water-based polyurethane.

Remove other loose paint with a stiff brush, working outside and wearing a protective mask. Then seal the piece.

Rattan

Gently scrub or douse with a garden hose. Let it dry in a sheltered area away from the sun. Rub with a clean cloth.

(NOTE: If your significant other lets you decorate with

bamboo, rattan, or wicker
pieces, count yourself lucky.)

Rush

Vacuum with a soft brush
attachment, or use a soft,
wide hand brush. Spot clean
spills with a damp cloth.

Suede

It's the rough undersurface
of leather. Vacuum with a
soft brush or use a soft
clothes brush. Use only made-
for-suede leather cleaners.

Freshen and restore with
suede brushes and soapstones.
Remove small spots with an
art gum eraser.

To lighten suede that's
darkened, buy a resin bag
from a sporting goods store
and pat it over the suede.
Brush away excess resin
with a suede brush, then a
clothes brush.

Keep suede away from sun
and heat. If you live in a

dry climate, make sure your
indoor air is not dry, which
can damage suede.

Veneer

Check to see if it's tight.
If there's a bubble, use a
crafts knife to make a small
slit that follows the wood
grain. Work in a small
amount of polyvinyl resin
glue (generally labeled for
veneers) with a knife.

Cover the patched bubble
with aluminum foil and
several layers of kraft paper
or fabric. Press with a dry,
hot iron. After 1 minute, turn
off the iron and leave it in
place several minutes.

Wicker

Vacuum wicker pieces with a
soft brush attachment. Wash
them with a brush dipped in
a mild detergent solution and
rinse. Or spray them with a
garden hose and dry in a
shaded, breezy area.

Upholstery Fabrics

If fabrics have a nap (I didn't know they got that tired, but it makes sense, what with people of all sizes sitting on them, day in, day out)—such as velvet, corduroy, or plush—vacuum with the nap. Determine the direction of the nap by running your hand over it. If the nap feels soft, you're running with the nap; if it feels rough, you're running against it.

If napped fabric looks streaked after vacuuming, run your hand, a clothing brush, or a dry towel over the fabric to smooth the nap. Deep-clean upholstered furniture every year or two, depending on the use, color, and pattern.

Commercial cleaning, do-it-yourself cleaning, and foam upholstery cleaners all work. Always test for dye stability.

Don't soak the fabric or the furniture structure.

Don't use soap products—sticky residues attract dirt and who knows what else.

Use cleaning products with a soil retardant to prevent future stains.

If frequent soiling is a problem, use a spray-silicon soil retardant that prevents stains from setting.

If the fabric was treated at the time of purchase, use compatible products. Follow the furniture manufacturer's directions.

Remove Pet Hair

Shave your pet from stem to stern and you'll have no more problems. (JOKE!) Use a clothes brush or a lint roller.

In a pinch, wrap masking tape around your hand, sticky side out, to pick up loose hair and fuzz. If the shedding seems excessive, call your veterinarian for advice.

Fabulous Furnishings

Give 'em the Slip
✳ ✳ ✳

Convert canvas or cotton duck painters' drop cloths into slipcovers. These drop cloths are washable, prehemmed, and come in a variety of sizes. Plus, they look hip and casual.

Purchase a cloth slightly larger than the sofa. Tuck the excess between cushions and allow it to pool on the floor.

If you iron slipcovers, press them on the wrong side to avoid damaging the surface.

When the slipcovers are in place, treat them with a stain-resistant finish.

To keep slipcovers from shifting, make a tuck-in furniture cover holder. Cut pieces of ½-inch-diameter PVC pipe slightly shorter than the seat back and side measurements of the cushions.

After tucking in the slipcover, slide the pipe pieces into the crevices as far as you can to hold the fabric in place. For chairs, use rolled magazines.

Spills happen. Gently blot—don't rub—immediately with a white cloth. Colored or printed paper towels may transfer dye or ink.

For larger spills, remove as much as possible with a spoon; blot up the rest.

Remove loose covers to clean. Leave fitted covers in place.

Wood Furniture
✳ ✳ ✳

Some dusting methods scatter dust into the air, where it floats until landing back on surfaces. You sure don't want that!

So dampen a cloth very slightly. Or use a soft electrostatic duster that traps dust.

Revive grimy wood furniture with equal parts of olive oil, denatured alcohol, lemon juice, and gum turpentine. Apply with a soft cloth; buff with a clean cloth. Avoid detergent and water and all-purpose cleaning sprays unless the furniture has a plastic coating, such as on kitchen tables.

Clean sticky spots (it's best not to even try and figure out who or what caused it) by wringing a cloth nearly dry and wiping. Rinse and dry with a clean, soft cloth.

Pass the Paste

Put a spoonful of wax the size of a golf ball in a square of cotton fabric. Wrap the fabric around the ball and knead until soft. (This is kind of fun and stress-relieving.) Rub in a circular motion, until the waxing is complete.

For a really deep shine, apply a second coat of wax the same way.

Maintain waxed furniture with a lamb's wool duster. Don't use liquid or aerosol polishes, which leave a hazy film.

Treating Treasures
*** * ***

You may need to deep-clean items like an old thrift-store table. First, use an oil soap and water to remove the grime. Rinse and dry well. Follow-up with #0000 steel wool dipped in naphtha or a wood cleaning product. Don't use mixtures with boiled linseed oil, turpentine, or white vinegars. These darken wood and attract dust. Instead, apply clear paste wax.

If a vintage piece has an unpleasant smell, air it outside on a warm, dry day. Shade it from the direct sun.

Pour talcum powder or baking soda over the surface to absorb odors. Vacuum to remove any residue.

Crumpled newspaper in drawers also absorbs odors.

If drawers stick, rub the upper edges with a white candle to loosen them.

Tips from Experts
✳ ✳ ✳

For treasured family heirlooms, use this cleaning routine recommended by Gracious Home, the New York City home furnishings store.

Clean

Yearly, apply Formby's Deep Cleaning Build-up Remover. Use fine-grain, #0000 steel wool, working with the grain, carefully following the product directions.

Restore

As needed, apply Howard Restor-A-Finish. Choose a shade closest to the wood stain. To restore original color from sun fading, apply the finish with #0000 steel wool. Work with the grain, using moderate pressure. Immediately wipe with a lint-free cloth.

Prevent Drying

Apply Howard Orange Oil or Feed-N-Wax beeswax monthly to prevent drying and cracking.

Additional Treatments

To clean heavily soiled wood furniture, use Lakeone Heavy-Duty Deep Cleaner. Remove old wax and dirt in sections with soft, dry cloths.

To revive discolored, hard-lacquered, or varnished finishes, apply Liberone Burnishing Cream Hard Finish Reviver to a clean, wax-free surface.

Soak a lint-free cloth with the burnishing cream and rub vigorously with the grain. Allow it to dry to a milky white powder; buff with a soft cloth.

If you suspect insect infestation (these little critters love to nibble on older furniture), apply Liberone Fongix SE; then apply a thin layer of buffing wax over the cleaned surface. Let dry and buff to the desired sheen.

Scratching the Surface

If the top surface of wood furniture is slightly scratched, apply paste wax or use a felt-tip furniture touch-up pen.

To treat deep scratches or gouges, use a wood filler or a colored filler wax stick available at hardware stores. Match it to the furniture color, applying it in several thin layers.

Wax yearly. First, dust with dusting or static cloths.

To polish hardware, remove it from the furniture piece. (Cleaning the hardware in place may ruin the surrounding wood finish.)

Clean with a brass cleaner and buff dry.

Sotheby's Suggestions

This famous furniture auction house has the following suggestions for keeping your wood furniture in tip-top shape:

- Keep furniture out of the direct sunlight.
- Maintain the humidity in your home at 45 to 50 percent and temperature at 65 to 68 degrees F. (You may need a humidifier.)
- Dust all your furniture at least weekly.
- Don't clean furniture with solvent or water. Both can remove the finish and can even change the patina. Also, don't use lemon oil or products with silicon or synthetic materials. Read labels on all products.
- Don't apply oil—it may give some varieties of wood a yellowish tinge.

Accessories, Artwork, and Collectibles

✳ ✳ ✳

Tabletop Tips

Put cloths between wood tabletops and lamps and accessories to prevent scratches. Or apply self-adhesive felt dots or glue a felt round to the bottoms of tabletop objects. Use watertight coasters.

Care and Cleaning

✳ ✳ ✳

Afghans and Throws

Launder most contemporary throws and afghans by machine, using a gentle cycle, cool water, and mild detergent. Tumble dry on the low setting.

Ivory, Horn, and Bone

To keep the warm white color, expose these pieces to natural light, but keep them away from sun and heat. Dust with a soft, dry cloth. Don't expose antique ivory, horn, or bone to water or cleansers.

Wipe ivory piano keys with a soft, damp cloth. If the keys are soiled, swipe the cloth over a cake of Ivory soap and rub the key in a lengthwise motion until the stain disappears entirely.

Dry with a soft cloth. (While you're at it, pretend you're a little kid again and play Chopsticks for fun.)

Artwork

Leave deep-cleaning and restoration to the professionals. Keep pieces away from direct sun, heat, cooking, and smoke.

Dust artwork with a soft, dry paint brush recommended for that purpose. Frequently dust picture frames with a soft, dry paintbrush or ostrich feather duster, taking care that the dust stays off the artwork.

Clean ornate frames with pure canned air that contains no cleaners or lubricants. It's available at many computer and art supply stores. Use the straw-like nozzle to reach small crevices.

Brass

A gentle patina is fine; tarnish isn't. If you prefer shiny brass, use a brass polish that contains wax. If you like a patina, use brass polish without wax. The brass will initially look shiny, then mellow. Keep brass out of the humidity and handle it as little as possible.

Candlesticks

Polish brass, silver, or other metal with cream polish formulated for the specific metal and a clean, soft cotton cloth. Paper towels can scratch the surface. Remove polish from crevices.

Wipe glass and crystal with a mild vinegar-and-water solution or with a clean, soft cotton rag moistened with commercial glass cleaner.

Soak grimy candlesticks in a vinegar-and-water bath or a denture solution. Rinse, dry, and polish with a lint-free cloth.

To remove wax from new candlesticks, not antique copper or brass ones, gently warm the holder with a hair dryer. Or place candlesticks upside down on a baking sheet and heat briefly in the oven on the lowest temperature setting. Remove wax and clean.

Ceiling and Wall Lights

Regularly dust ceiling lights, track lights, canister lights, and sconces with a feather duster or electrostatic duster.

Fabulous Furnishings

For sconces and track lights, turn off the electricity at the breaker box. Wipe the fixtures with a slightly damp cloth. Dry thoroughly before turning the power back on.

Wash most removable shades in warm water with mild detergent. Rinse and dry them before reinserting them.

Ceramics

Wash glazed ceramics in lukewarm water with mild detergent. Rinse and dry thoroughly.

Wipe unglazed ceramics with a damp cloth. Don't immerse.

Clocks

Follow the care instructions that you would for furniture made from the same material.

Keep clocks on level surfaces, away from temperature changes, direct sunlight, and heat vents.

Place tall case clocks—such as grandfather clocks—in stable corners where they're least likely to be tipped over or knocked into. Clock repair shops sell devices to secure tall case clocks to the wall.

Copper

Unsealed items will discolor (oxidation turns metal green). Use copper polish. Keep items away from moisture and humidity.

Crystal Chandeliers

Use a feather duster to dust them regularly. (See cleaning tips in Chapter 2.)

Decorative Trims

Remove stitched-on trim from upholstery, pillows, or window treatments. Place decorative trims in a mesh laundry bag. Fluff in the dryer on air cycle. Hand-stitch trims back into place. Don't remove trim that is securely attached or glued on.

Fabulous Furnishings

Pillows

Take off the removable outer shells. Most upholstery fabrics require dry cleaning. Some cotton fabrics, such as bedspread chenille, chintz, and other plain weaves, can be gently machine-washed in cool water and then dried on low heat.

(DANGER: Don't remove those pillow tags, or the Pillow Tag Team will come after you. I don't know why pillow tags say that, do you?)

Spot clean with a commercial stain remover to eliminate minor soil. Follow directions. Test clean first on an inconspicuous area.

Let professionals deal with heavily accented pillows. Embellishments are often the most fragile and least colorfast parts of pillows.

For washable fringed pieces or those with sturdy button or stud trims, place the pillow cover inside a pillow protector to machine wash on the gentle cycle in cool water. Remove the pillow immediately to prevent trims from rusting or bleeding. Dry on the coolest setting.

Quilts

Don't dry-clean quilts, and launder them as little as possible. When they require washing, check with quilting or fabric shops to purchase laundry detergent formulated especially for quilts. Wash them in cool water on gentle. Dry on the low or air cycle. To display folded quilts and textiles, rearrange and refold the pieces often to prevent a permanent crease and to avoid damage from light along edges.

Table and Floor Lamps

Unplug the lamp and remove the shade and bulb. Dust or damp-wipe the light bulb.

Fabulous Furnishings

Place the lampshades on a solid surface. Many are made with glue that water dissolves. Vacuum with a soft brush, or use a feather duster or soft, clean paintbrush. The lanolin in a lamb's wool duster may stain the shade fabric.

Dry-clean silk and antique shades or those with delicate trim.

Wipe metal and plastic shades with a slightly damp cloth. Dry immediately.

Metal shades may rust, especially at rivet points, and plastic shades may water spot.

Brass, Chrome, and Nickel

Dust with a soft cloth. Polish with a cleaner formulated for the metal.

Ceramic, China, Glass, Marble, or Plastic

Dust lamp bases with a damp cloth and warm detergent solution. Rinse with another cloth dampened with clear water and dry.

Area Rugs and Floor Coverings
✳ ✳ ✳

Basic Care

Small area rugs are a pain to vacuum. Take them outside and shake vigorously until the dust and dirt are gone. (Just pretend you're a dancer for a minute—it's a lot more fun that way.)

You can also hang rugs over a clothesline or sturdy outdoor furniture and beat them with a broom to remove dirt. (The beating technique is a great stress-reducer, and quite invigorating.)

Hang wet rugs on a drying rack, slatted picnic table, or stack of clean bricks on a porch, patio, or breezeway. To dry small rugs made from synthetic fibers, lay them on a small worktable or counter that is protected by a drop cloth, old sheets, or towels.

Pet Problems

When pet hair accumulates in a rug, brush the rug vigorously with a stiff utility brush. Brush with the nap until dirt and hair stop coming out.

Attack urine and fecal stains with an enzymatic cleaner that breaks down stain and odor. If your pet is soiling areas often, check with your veterinarian to see if your four-legged friend has a medical problem that could be the cause.

Special Cases
* * *

Antique, Hand-Knotted, and Oriental Rugs

Use special care with delicate vintage, antique, or hand-knotted rugs. Protect from vacuuming by laying a piece of nylon screen over the rug, weighting it around the edges. Vacuum over the screen. The dirt will be removed while the screen protects the rug.

Vacuum new Oriental rugs as you would carpet. Rotate rugs to ensure even wear; sun causes fading.

Immediately treat wine and other beverage spills with club soda; use baking soda to soak up gravy, sauces, and liquid foods.

Rush, Seagrass, Sisal, and Natural Materials

These may have an open weave, allowing dirt to sift through to the floor below. Vacuum often, removing the rug occasionally to vacuum the floor.

If possible, take the rug outside and gently beat it to loosen dirt trapped between the fibers. Many of these rugs are reversible. If yours are, flip them over each time you

Fabulous Furnishings

vacuum for even wear. To clean discolorations or stains on a room-size natural fiber rug, leave the rug in place, protecting the floor beneath with a plastic drop cloth and towel.

Scrub the stains with a soft brush dipped in a detergent solution. Rinse thoroughly with clear water.

Fur and Sheepskin

Shake unscented talcum powder over the rug and leave for several hours. Brush the talcum powder through the hair; shake it out.

Repeat this process several times, depending on the length of the fur.

Woven and Braided Rugs

Check for stitching breaks before and after cleaning. Check labels to see if small rugs are washable.

Put washable rugs in a zippered pillowcase or mesh laundry bag. Wash in cool water on the gentle cycle.

Window Treatments

* * *

Metal and Vinyl Blinds

Dust with a cloth or blind-dusting tool.

Quick Clean

Wear rubber gloves; topped with cotton gloves. Mix 1 teaspoon ammonia in 1 quart water. Dip gloved fingers in the solutions and run them along the slats with your thumb under each slat.

Wood

Dust with a soft cloth or blind-dusting tool. Soiling can be removed from painted blinds by using a damp cloth. Treat stained-wood blinds with lemon oil or any other wood preservative.

Curtains and Draperies

Check the label before laundering ready-made curtains. If they're washable, remove hooks, rings, and any other hardware. Unless the directions say otherwise, machine wash on a short, gentle cycle, using cool water and mild detergent. Dry on low and remove immediately.

Fiberglass

These still exist in some homes, and are sometimes sold in stores featuring vintage or mid-20th-century textiles. They require special care and handling.

Never machine wash or dry-clean fiberglass material. Glass fibers will break away during the agitation cycle.

Hand wash these items, wearing rubber gloves, in a large laundry tub—not a bathtub—filled with water and detergent. Rinse well.

Lace

Remove dust by tumbling curtains in the dryer on the air cycle. Many new lace curtains are hand or machine washable. Follow the label directions or gently wash in cool water. Wash sheers in the same way as you would lace curtains.

Window Shades
* * *
Bamboo

Unroll the shade and lay it flat. Weight each end. Wash one side with a sponge dipped in a mild detergent solution. Rinse with a clean, damp cloth and dry. Hang to dry.

Outdoor Furniture
* * *
Basic Care

Most pieces can be cleaned with mild liquid hand-dishwashing detergent and water, then

Fabulous Furnishings

rinsed and dried. Products for cleaning, polishing, and protecting vehicle surfaces are made to withstand weathering and will work on most types of outdoor furniture.

Aluminum

Use a detergent solution, add 2 tablespoons of lemon juice, vinegar, or cream of tartar. Polish with a soapy steel wool pad, rinse, and dry.

Bamboo, Wicker, and Rattan

Marine varnish provides some protection when these materials are exposed to the weather.

Nylon and Vinyl Webbing

Replace worn strapping with kits from home centers or hardware stores. Clean regularly; a buildup of soil or suntan lotions can cause fungus to grow.

Painted Metal

Baked-on enamel is the most durable; paint or enamel applied directly to the metal is the least durable. Apply paste wax and then polish.

Plastics

These have lacquered resin finishes that help protect them against ultraviolet rays, rain, and salt spray. Plastics are easily scratched by strong alkalis or abrasives. Apply wax or a protective finish to the untreated surfaces.

Teak

Luckily, teak resists decay, termites, wood-boring insects, water, acids, and metal stains. Wood exposed to the sun gradually bleaches to silvery gray. Periodic oiling slows graying, darkening the wood with a soft sheen.

Girls Just Wanna Have Clean

4

LOVE THAT LAUNDRY

Having clean laundry makes you feel so good, so organized, like you really accomplished something. But you can only celebrate if your laundry comes out OK.

By that, I mean that your red towels don't turn your hubby's shorts pink, your fuzzy blue sweater lint doesn't clog up the dryer lint trap, or you don't shrink your best size-12 blouse into a size 2 even Kate Moss couldn't wear. With the great hints coming up, you'll avoid these laundry disasters. So don't dare skip this chapter! It's even fun to read.

Get With the Plan, Man—Installation
✳ ✳ ✳

Location

If you're lucky enough to put the laundry center where you want it, consider the sites below.

Basement

This area requires climbing steps while carrying baskets, but keeps your living space clear. Spills, splashes, or overflow may do less damage.

Plus, you'll burn off extra calories by running up and down the stairs. Include a scrub sink for hand-laundry. A drying rack or indoor clothesline is good for drip-drying and saving energy.

Bathroom/Dressing Room

Plumbing is handy—convenient for doing daily laundry. But leaks could damage floors and ceilings if it's on the upper level.

Bedroom Area

Having a washer and dryer in a utility closet saves steps. But leaks could damage carpets, floors, and ceilings if it's on an upper floor.

Kitchen

A laundry in or near the kitchen is good for handy plumbing and easy multitasking chores. Cabinets provide storage space for supplies.

You Get to Shop Again!
✳ ✳ ✳

Choosing a Washer/Dryer

Washers and dryers are 24 to 33 inches wide. For loading and unloading, allow 36 to 42 inches in the front. Front-loading models may differ in size. Stacked units occupy less than 33 inches of floor space and fit in small spaces. They're perfect for small spaces, or apartments or

Love That Laundry

townhomes with limited square feet.

Some machines have optional risers that raise them 15 to 19 inches off the floor, reducing bending or stooping. Front-loaders are more accessible to wheelchair users.

Master Your Washer

Consider capacity and load. Capacity depends on the wash basket size. Ranges are compact (1.7 to 2.3 cubic feet (cf); medium (2.1 to 2.5 cf); large (2.7 to 3 cf); and extra large (3.1 or more cf).

Basic washers have one to four agitations (that means moving speeds, not that they're upset) and spin speeds, plus regular, permanent-press, and delicate cycles. Many higher-end models offer preset options, plus the choice of heavy-duty, presoak, and prewash cycles.

Water temperature presets are hot wash/cold rinse, warm/cold, and cold/cold. Higher-end models offer more combos. Controls are mechanical, with rotary knobs and push buttons, or electrical, with various conveniences, sometimes even including digital displays.

High-efficiency units save water and energy. Check the appliance labels for the Energy Star rating.

Consider delay-start features, automatic water-level controls, internal water heaters, stainless-steel or polypropylene tubs (smooth and rustproof), and spin cycles of 700 to 1,600 revolutions per minute (spinning loads nearly dry, saving time and energy).

Doubts About Dryers?

The size of the drum determines the capacity. Ranges are compact (2 to 4 cf); medium (4 to 5.8 cf); large (5.9 to 6.9 cf); and extra large (7 or more cf).

Conquering Clean

✳ ✳ ✳

Plumbing and Wiring

Washers need drains, hot and cold water lines, and 20-amp small-appliance circuits. Electric dryers require 120-volt circuits.

Some models condense moisture into a drip pan without venting. Gas dryers need a gas supply line, outside venting (maximum of 50 feet), and 20-amp small-appliance circuits.

Units must be on independent, grounded circuits. (If this is as confusing to you as it is to me, you might want to hire a pro.)

Install an emergency shut-off valve on washers and regularly check hoses for wear and tight connections. (Or hire a professional to accomplish this.)

Room Lighting

Uniform, glare-free light is important to inspect, sort, and fold laundry. You'll quickly catch laundry boo-boos on your family's clothes (and hide them and accuse family members of losing them before they blame you).

For dark laundry centers, as in a basement or windowless space, use true-color incandescent bulbs that mimic sunlight.

Storage

Install shelving or cabinets to keep supplies handy. Wall or back-of-door hooks hold an ironing board out of the way, if you iron. (I prefer not to, and do so only in desperate measures, like clothes for a wedding or a fun girls' night out on the town.)

Space Savers

Change a closet into a laundry room with stackable

storage units. Install racks for laundry supplies on the back of the closet door.

Install a closet rod for clothes that drip dry, or that you hang directly out of the dryer. Use double rods if you hang primarily shirts and slacks. Add a rack for socks.

(You get bonus points if you can wash and dry socks and come out with completely matched pairs, and no lonely leftovers.)

If space allows, build a counter for folding and sorting. Also, put an ironing board and iron in the laundry room. If the room doesn't have a storage closet, hang the ironing board from a heavy-duty storage hook.

Get This Stuff!

* * *

All products should be kept out of children's reach on upper shelves or in locked cabinets. (Keep products off the washer and dryer; drips could damage exterior surfaces.)

- Ammonia, nonsudsing
- Antistatic dryer sheets
- Baking soda
- Bleach, chlorine and color-safe
- Color remover like prewash stain removers, including towelettes. (Now, isn't that a pretty, dainty word? Kind of sounds French.)
- Dry-cleaning fluid or petroleum-based pretreatment solvent spot lifter
- Dry-cleaning kit for the dryer. (I still don't get how these work, but they're super and can save you tons of money. And I guess I don't have to know everything, anyway.)
- Enzyme presoak product (these contain amylase for starch, protease for protein, and lipase for fats). Most laundry detergents contain enzymes.

Love That Laundry

- Gentle detergent for fine washables (like Victoria's Secret undies)
- Laundry detergent
- Oxygen detergent boosters
- Paint remover
- Petroleum jelly
- Rust removers
- Spray sizing and starch
- White bar soap
- White paper towels
- White vinegar
- Special treats for you to eat while you do the laundry (Have a juicy, gossipy magazine to read when you finish this task. Add a few nibbles—pretzels if you're going for salty, caramels if you want something sweet.)

Let Your Whole Family Join the Fun
✳ ✳ ✳

It's time they helped out. Delegate a laundry chore to each family member. Give simple tasks, such as folding socks, to young children.

One- or Two-Person Household

Doing the laundry weekly is plenty, unless you wash uniforms, or work or gym clothes. If dress shirts and suits are part of your attire, take them to the cleaners. This can get expensive—look for coupons in your local shopper or paper, or buy a coupon book.

Three or More In Household

Do one load every morning (or every other morning) and fold clothes at night.

Train family members to put dirty clothing in their own personal hamper. Get a different style or color for every family member. Place three additional hampers in the laundry area for sorting dark, light, and special-care items. (This is important, believe me. Sort, sort, sort is now my mantra, after decades of laundry disasters. Perhaps I was born without the laundry gene, or this is some type of domestic rebellion I can't control.)

Goin' for Clean
✻ ✻ ✻

Common Fabrics
Acrylic Knit

Normally machine washable. Read the label—check for proper drying. Some knits keep shape best if dried flat.

Cotton

This fabric is known for holding up well to home laundering. Remove any cotton items from the dryer promptly to reduce wrinkling (and save you time ironing). Press with spray starch for the crispness of a professionally laundered shirt. (Or, if you've found enough money in the sofa cushions, just send them out.)

Cotton Blend

Dry these items on the permanent-press or low cycle and remove immediately to reduce wrinkling. Touch up with steam iron; starch for a professional look. Spray on starch is convenient and fun to spray.

Linen

These may be dry-cleaned or hand washed. Read care labels. If pressing, steam iron for a crisp look.

Polyester

Read the label. Normally machine washed (cool) and dried (low) is best. Read to see if air-drying is recommended. Touch up with a cool iron—never hot—only if necessary.

(If you iron it with a hot iron, the iron will either stick to the fabric or melt it. Trust me on this.)

Silk

Professional cleaning is best. Some silks are hand or machine-washable, but it's nerve-racking because these items are so pricey. NEVER machine dry.

Wool Knit

Wool can be dry-cleaned, but check the label. If hand washable, use cool water and detergent for fine washables. Dry-clean to retain shape, or use an in-dryer kit.

Avoid Laundry Mishaps
* * *

If you have doubts about colorfastness, wash separately in a low-water setting or a mini basket if your machine has one. Or mix a small amount of detergent with a cup of warm water. Moisten an inner seam or inconspicuous spot. Rub with a clean, dry, white towel. If color comes off, launder the garment separately.

Check pockets for pens, crayons, coins, tissues, etc. Tissues can come apart in the wash and be a real mess to pick off everything. (However, this could be a good task for the family-member culprit who left the tissues in his or her pocket.) Be vigilant about crayons and lipstick. If they survive the wash, they melt in the dryer, staining clothing.

Pretreat soiled shirt collars and cuffs with a prewash stain removal product or liquid laundry detergent.

Use the recommended amount of detergent. Too much means extra rinsing; too little may not clean well. Don't judge by how much suds you see. Most formulas are made for low-sudsing (although suds are pretty and always remind me of clouds).

Love That Laundry

Check water temperature. Detergents work best in warm or hot water. Use cold water only for items that might fade or that are just lightly soiled.

Dissolve detergent in warm water first. If your model has it, use an automatic water-temperature control for maximum efficiency.

Turn fine washables inside out and use the delicate or knit setting if you machine-wash delicate blouses, panty hose, tights, etc.

Stain Stoppers
* * *

Inspect clothes before both washing and drying. If a stain remains after laundering, treat with a stain removal product and rewash.

Blotting draws the stain away from fabric; rubbing pushes it into fabric. One exception is: A gentle rubbing motion under running water helps remove dried food, protein, or oil stains from denim-weight fabric or cotton and cotton-polyester blends.

Don't use terry cloth towels or dark cloths when blotting—lint and dye transfer from dark colors may make things worse.

Wash heavily stained items separately to avoid transferring stains.

Don't use hot water on stains of unknown origin. It sets protein stains.

Gone with the Stains
* * *

If a fabric is dry-clean only, blot off excess and take it to the cleaners as soon as possible. Point out stains and spots so they can be specially treated.

Love That Laundry

The following tips are for general home laundry. You might want to make a copy of this and put it in your laundry room.

Baby Formula

Pretreat or soak stains with a product containing enzymes. Soak for at least 30 minutes. Launder normally. (Always launder infants' clothing in mild detergent for baby clothes.)

Blood

(Yuck. Watch out for those brand-new razors.)

For fresh stains, soak in cold water (hot water will set this stain). Then launder with detergent and an oxygen booster.

For dried stains, pretreat or soak in warm water with an enzyme product; launder. If the stain remains, use a bleach safe for the fabric.

Butter

(Someone's not watching their cholesterol!) Pretreat with a prewash stain remover or liquid laundry detergent. Wash using the hottest water safe for the fabric.

Chocolate

Pretreat stains with an enzyme product or prewash stain remover; launder. If the stain remains, rewash with bleach safe for the fabric.

Coffee or Tea

Pretreat these stains with stain remover or liquid laundry detergent. Or rub them with bar soap.

Then launder them as usual. Rewash them if needed.

Collar and Cuff Soil

Pretreat with a general laundry stain remover, liquid laundry detergent, or a paste of detergent and water.

Love That Laundry

Crayon

(Uh-oh. Somebody's been artistic again!) For a few spots, scrape off excess with a dull knife. Place stained area between white paper towels and press with a warm iron. Reposition paper towels as the crayon is absorbed.
To remove stain, place spot facedown on several layers of white paper towels.

Sponge the back with a prewash stain remover or cleaning fluid. Blot with white paper towels. Dry naturally before laundering with detergent and chlorine or color-safe bleach.

For an entire load affected by crayons (this may have called for a group time-out of more than an hour), pretreat or soak in a product containing enzymes, or chlorine or color-safe bleach. Using the hottest water safe for the fabric, rewash with detergent and 1 cup baking soda.

Diesel Fuel or Gasoline

Use extra caution—these stains make clothing flammable. Use only detergent-based stain removers, not solvent-based ones. Air items thoroughly. Don't place in the dryer if there's a fuel smell.

Fruit Juices

Soak in cold water using fabric-safe bleach.

Grass

Pretreat with a stain remover or liquid laundry detergent. Launder using the hottest water safe for the fabric.
For heavy stains, place items facedown on several layers of white paper towels. Apply the cleaning fluid to the back of the stain. Replace towels as the stain is absorbed. Let dry; rinse and launder.

Gravy

Pretreat or soak with product containing enzymes. Soak for

30 minutes if the stain is dry. Launder as usual.

(HINT: Don't make gravy that often, maybe just on Thanksgiving. It's fattening, it makes bad spots that are hard to get out, and it has a lot of cholesterol. Plus, if you have gravy, chances are you're going to have to peel a mountainous pile of potatoes to mash to go with it.)

Ink

Common inks, including ballpoint, felt-tip, and liquid, are almost impossible to remove, but try pretreatments.

Lipstick

Hope this stain was on your clothes—not your significant other's! Sponge or soak using cool water; pretreat. Launder with bleach.

Mustard

Pretreat with stain remover. Launder with bleach.

Nail Polish

Trying to remove this may be dreaming the impossible dream. But if you're up for it, try this method (not for acetate or triacetate fabric). Place the stain facedown on layers of white paper towels. Apply polish remover to back of stain. Replace the towels as they accept the polish. Repeat, rinse, and launder.

Olive Oil

Mamma mia! Pretreat with a prewash stain remover or liquid laundry detergent. Wash using the hottest water safe for the fabric.

Paint (Oil-Based)

If the paint label recommends a thinner, use that solvent for stain removal. Or sponge with turpentine; rinse. Pretreat with a prewash stain remover, bar soap, or laundry detergent. Rinse, launder, or take to a dry cleaner.

Love That Laundry

Paint (Water-Based)

Rinse the fabric in warm water while the stains are wet; launder. For dried paint, take the item to a dry cleaner.

Perspiration

Apply ammonia to fresh stains or white vinegar to old stains; rinse. Launder using the hottest water safe for the fabric.

Pesticides

Never wash pesticide-soiled items with other laundry.

Plain Old Dirt

Allow the mud to dry. Brush off as much as possible before washing. For really tough stains, use a prespot product, then soak in laundry detergent for at least 30 minutes; launder.

Red Wine

Sponge or soak the stain, using cool water. Pretreat with a stain remover or liquid laundry detergent. Launder with bleach. (It may be easier to just switch to white wine.)

Scorching

This may be beyond hope. Launder using chlorine bleach, if it's safe for the fabric. Otherwise, soak the item in color-safe bleach and the hottest water safe for the fabric; then launder.

Tomato Sauce

Apply prewash stain remover or liquid laundry detergent. Wash with liquid laundry detergent, using safe bleach and water temperature.

Urine, Vomit, Mucus, Feces

(Now here's a laundry task that might be the perfect one to delegate to your hubby or significant other.)

Launder using chlorine bleach (which disinfects), color-safe bleach, or oxygen booster.

Wax

Use a dull knife to scrape off as much as possible. For remaining wax, place between paper towels and press with a warm iron. Replace towels as the wax is absorbed.

Don't Be a Load
✳ ✳ ✳

Washer

Never overload; it leaves less room for water, limiting effective cleaning and damaging fabrics.

"Walking" machines that shift out of position and go noisily off balance during spin cycles are a result of overloading.

(This is really a scary sound at night, especially if you're alone and have just watched a horror movie.)

Consistent overloading can bend the washer's frame or damage the motor, eventually requiring repair.

Check the loading instructions on the machine's lid. The best order is detergent, water, and then items to be washed. This prevents oversudsing and minimizes any damage from full-strength detergents.

Dryer

Check the lint trap before each load. A full trap reduces efficiency and is a fire hazard.

Overloading the dryer results in poor air flow, taking more time and energy to dry your clothes. Overweight loads can result in misalignments of the dryer drum, which may cause damage needing repair or replacement.

Do several smaller loads rather than one large, crammed one. Clothing needs room for air to circulate. Save energy with a shorter drying time. Don't put the lightweight items in the same load as the heavy items; the lighter ones may shrink.

Drying times depend on the load size, garment weight, and fiber content. For example, six cotton bath towels that weigh 5 pounds dry in 40 minutes.

A permanent-press load, also 5 pounds, takes 30 to 40 minutes. (The great thing about the permanent press setting is that usually you don't have to iron these clothes.)

(These statistics remind me of the ACT and SAT test questions you take in high school. One that still haunts me is: If you have a coal bin 5 feet wide and 2 feet deep, how much coal can you fit into it? I've always thought that question was important, since I've had to fill so many coal bins in my journey through life so far.)

After the Laundry's Over
* * *

Overall Grayness

This could be caused by low water temperature, incorrect sorting (resulting in dirt or color transfer), or not enough detergent. To solve this problem, increase the wash cycle temperature.

Sort heavily soiled from lightly soiled items and carefully sort by color. Use the right amount of detergent with bleach.

Uneven Grayness

Usually this is caused by not using enough detergent. Rewash with the correct amount and the hottest water safe for the fabric.

Yellowing

Buildup of body soil may cause yellowing. Use a detergent booster or bleach safe for fabric type. (And stay in air-conditioning as much as possible.)

Blue Stains

Detergent or fabric softener may not be dissolving. If detergent causes the problem, soak the garment in a plastic container using 1 cup white vinegar to 1 quart water. Soak for 1 hour; rinse and launder.

To avoid these stains, add the detergent and turn on warm water before adding laundry. If using fabric softener, rub stains with bar soap. Rinse and launder.

Powder Residue

Causes include undissolved detergent or low water temperature. Add detergent and dissolve it in warm water before adding laundry.

Stiffness or Fading

Hard water may cause stiffness and fading. Use liquid detergent or add a water softener product.

Lint

This can be caused by mixing items such as bath towels and napped velour or corduroy, a clogged washer lint filter, a full dryer lint screen, or tissues left in the pockets of garments. Rewash separately.

Pilling

This is a wear problem of some synthetic and permanent-press fabrics. Use a lint brush or roller with masking tape to remove pills. Adding a fabric softener may help.

Shrinkage

Irreversible damage. (All of Humpty Dumpty's men can't put this one together again. You may have to donate that former size-12 blouse that's now a size 4 to your daughter.) Avoid by following labels' instructions, or wash in warm water and rinse in cold. Reduce drying time and remove garments when slightly damp.

Worn Areas

Place delicate items, such as fine lingerie or hose, in mesh bags made for washing delicates to avoid abrasion from other garments or the agitator.

Special Laundering

✳ ✳ ✳

Antique Linens

Very old lace or fabrics may tear if washed. Linens at antiques fairs usually are already cleaned and pressed, but if you find fabrics at a garage sale or antiques shop, you'll want to clean them. Hold fabrics to the light to check for worn spots, tears, broken threads, and holes.

Test a piece of embroidery for colorfastness by gently dabbing the thread on the back of the piece with a damp white cloth. If no color comes off on the cloth, you can wash the piece safely.

It's usually safe to machine-wash embroidered dresser scarves, pillowcases, hand towels, and table runners from the 1930s and '40s if the fabric is not worn or fragile. Press while damp.

To clean fine linen or pieces with handmade lace, fringe, or crocheted edging, presoak for 15 minutes in clear water to loosen up the dirt. Gently swish linens in the warm water containing nonabrasive, phosphate-free, mild detergent.

Bleach can easily damage these fragile fibers, so don't use it. Rinse twice in cool, clear water.

Old stains may be impossible to remove, but try presoaking them in an enzyme cleaner. Or add nonchlorine bleach to the wash water.

The old-fashioned method for bleaching white fabric is to rub lemon juice and salt on a stain. Hang on a clothesline or spread the fabric out to dry in the sun. (Pretend you're a pioneer while you do it, just for the heck of it.)

Wash chenille in the washing machine and dry it in the dryer. If you need to iron it, lay the fabric, tufted side down, on a well-padded ironing board and use the cotton setting.

Caution: Danger Zone!

If you feel compelled to iron and spray starch all your sheets, hankies, and your hubby's boxer shorts and T-shirts, you may want to:

1. Decrease your caffeine intake—no cheating with soda pop—some kinds have more caffeine than coffee.
2. Go to more parties.
3. Throw your own party.
4. Take up a fun hobby that relaxes you, like belly-dancing or easy cross-stitching. (Just be careful if you cross-stitch in the morning in your pajamas, not to accidentally stitch the project to your jammies, as I once did.)

Best Bedding Bets
* * *

Change and launder sheets and pillowcases weekly. (Remember, dust mites feast on human skin. You don't even want to think about these! They even look scary not magnified 100 times.) Protect pillows with washable zip-on covers. Wash sheets in warm water, and use nonchlorine bleach when needed. Wash all-cotton spreads, blankets, and coverlets in cold water. Naturally refresh pillows, comforters, and duvets by airing them outside on a sunny day.

Love That Laundry

Even in large dryers, only twin comforters can fit. You'll need to take larger ones to the dry cleaners.

For allergy control, put your pillows, comforters, mattress, and box spring in impermeable covers with zippers. Vacuum the mattress and box springs before you cover them. (These covers don't work on down products.)

Some bedding is made with allergy-resistant fibers that are machine-washable.

Wash bedcoverings that have not been encased in hot water. Wash covers twice a year in warm water.

Remove pet hairs from dry-clean-only bedcovers and throws by placing them in the dryer with an anti-static dryer sheet. Run the dryer on low or no heat for 20 to 30 minutes. Clean the lint trap.

Blouses, Dresses, and Dress Shirts

Read care labels for instructions and water temperature. Save time by immediately removing cotton-blend clothing from the dryer, so maybe you won't have to iron it. (Whoopee!)

Children's Sleepwear

Never use chlorine bleach on flame-resistant fabrics. It reduces effectiveness of the treatment chemicals and might ruin treated fabrics. Follow the care instructions.

Electric Blankets

These can be gently laundered to extend blanket life and keep them fresh.
- Disconnect electrical cord.
- Check the care label.
- Pretreat soiled areas.
- Fill the washer with warm water to the highest level.
- Add liquid laundry detergent; agitate briefly.

Love That Laundry

- Load evenly; soak for 15 minutes—don't agitate.
- Set for 2 minutes of gentle agitation; start the washer.
- Put three or four clean, dry bath towels into the dryer.
- Load a blanket the into dryer with warm towels.
- Set timed drying cycle for 20 minutes; start dryer. Check after 10 minutes. Continue only if the blanket is sopping wet.
- Remove slightly damp blanket (overdrying damages wiring and causes shrinkage).
- Hang the blanket over two lines, or lay flat, until dry.
- Check for worn or frayed fabric, scorching, loose connections, or damaged, worn, or missing tapes, cords, or wiring.
- If damage appears, discard the electric blanket.

Quilts

Quilts can be professionally dry-cleaned by a laundry that specializes in fine linens. Launder vintage quilts as little as possible. Before laundering, check with quilting or fabric shops to purchase laundry products formulated especially for washing quilts. Dry on low temperature.

Durable quilts for everyday use can be machine washed if they fit into the washer.

Towels

Good-quality bath towels can last 10 years with proper care. (That's longer than some marriages.)

Wash and dry new towels before use to remove excess dye. Launder them separately, not with clothes, for sanitary reasons.

Use warm water to wash towels; don't overdry. It destroys the integrity of individual cotton fibers. (And there's nothing more disappointing than cotton with no integrity.)

Love That Laundry

Avoid waxy buildup—two terrible words—from fabric softener; use it only once every three or four washings.

Keep dark-colored towels separate for the first few washings because colors may bleed. (This happened to me with black towels and it turned everything gray.)

Wash similar colors together. Use color-safe bleach.

Wash white towels with other white items to avoid subtle discoloration over time. Occasionally bleach white towels if needed. If you hang towels to dry, shake them while wet and again when dry to fluff the terry loops.

Maximize towel absorbency by adding a cup of white vinegar to the rinse water once a month. Dry as usual. (Vinegar is good for removing excess detergent.)

Hand Laundry
* * *

Some fine washables, including delicate lingerie or old lace, are best done by hand.

Use a mild laundry detergent or product for hand washables, such as knits or sweaters.

Products with high alkaline content are not recommended for cotton hand-washables. Read the label.

Fill a sink or small tub with water and detergent. Soak the garment; never scrub or twist. Rinse with clear water.

Gently squeeze out excess water. Don't wring. (I know it's fun, but twisting can stretch or deform the shape of fine knits.) Roll heavy garments in white cotton terry towels to remove excess water.

Love That Laundry

Ironing Techniques
* * *

(True Confession: I hate ironing so much that I usually don't buy anything that has to be ironed. I do have a cheap one to use in case of dire wrinkle emergencies.)

Irons range from $10 to more than $100 for specialty ones. They come in several types.

Dry Iron

The most basic and inexpensive iron has a flat soleplate, a heat-generating element, and several heat settings. (This is what I have—surprised?)

Steam Iron

This is the most common iron, but features vary by price and manufacturer.

Iron with Variable Steam

Adjusts the steam released.

Burst/Surge of Steam

These models produce concentrated outflow.

Vertical Steam Models

This type of iron produces steam while the iron is upright, allowing its use as a steamer for clothes on hangers. It's kind of handy—especially when you travel.

Fabulous Features
* * *

Automatic Shutoff

This turns it off when it's horizontal for a certain time.

Cord Swivel

(Sounds like a new dance step, doesn't it?) Some irons allow cord movement in any position, reducing wire stress within the cord and preventing the cord getting in the way.

Cordless

Some cordless irons warm on heat plates, allowing free movement while ironing.

Nonstick Soleplate

This nonstick surface makes cleaning starch buildup easier.

Variable Heat Settings

Top-of-the-line irons include more temperature settings for a wide variety of fabrics.

Steam Iron Care

Before using, clean the vents, following the manufacturer's instructions. This usually involves filling the water well, plugging in the iron, setting it on the highest temperature, and allowing it to sit upright for about three minutes to build up steam. Turn off the iron, unplug it, and pour out the water. If your iron has a "self-clean" setting, switch to it after unplugging. If you have extremely hard water, use bottled spring water or a half-and-half mix of untreated tap water and distilled water. Never use 100 percent distilled water unless the instructions require it.

Don't use household water softeners; they may cause the iron to leak or spit.

If you enjoy sweet-smelling sheets or garments, spray with scented water made for ironing. Use it in place of tap water in your steam iron. After using your iron, drain it well.

Soleplate Care

Do not iron over metal zippers, snaps, hooks, or pins. Occasionally wipe with a cloth dampened in warm water with mild hand-dishwashing detergent. Rinse with a damp cloth; dry with a soft cloth. Never use abrasives, such as scouring pads, which scratch. Always store the iron upright on the heel plate.

Ironing Boards
* * *

Ironing boards range from $15 to $800 for professional-quality models from specialty home stores. (Rather than spending $800 on an ironing board, a getaway weekend might do you more good and be more fun too.)

A standard full-size ironing board with a clean, well-fitting cover ensures the best results. Choose a medium-priced, easy-to-fold model.

(WARNING: Wrestling with cheap ironing boards is painful and humiliating. They always win. The easiest to use ironing boards are adjustable metal X-leg types.)

Look for adjustable models that allow comfortable use either when sitting or standing. The ironing surface should be at hip level. Some affordable boards provide cord holders to prevent tangles and iron rests to prevent scorching.

Select an ironing board with thick cotton padding to reduce overheating and wrinkling. Pad covers come in many patterns and colors and in fabrics with nonstick coatings to make starch cleanup easy.

Pressing for Dressing

Avoid a shiny look when pressing wool or dark fabrics by using a press cloth, a clean cotton dish towel, or a soleplate attachment.

Starch or Sizing?

Use spray starch for natural fabrics such as cotton. Spray sizing is for synthetics. Spray lightly from several inches away. Waxy residue means the iron is too hot; flick away excess and reduce heat. For a soft finish, spritz with water; iron lightly.

Close the zippers and press the inside flaps with the very tip of the iron. Unzip and iron lightly along the fabric.

Blouses and Dresses

Follow the instructions on the label (sometimes on the back of the label). Large areas of fabric require using the wide end of the ironing board.

Iron embroidered designs by laying the garment facedown on a terry cloth towel and pressing with a burst of steam. Cover delicate buttons by placing the bowl of a spoon over each one and ironing all around them.

For a French cuff (ohh-la-la) use a sleeve board or roll a towel into the sleeve and iron the cuff. Iron the shirt body, doing one front panel at a time. Repress the collar.

Slacks

Lay the pockets on the ironing board and press flat. Fit the waistband around the end of the board, and rotate the slacks as you press the waistband and pants top.

Lay pants flat, with one leg on top of the other. Align inseams with outer seams.

Iron the inside of the bottom leg by folding back the top leg. Flip and repeat to iron the other side.

With the inseams aligned, press the outside of each leg separately. If you're using a steam iron, use a short burst of steam to help set the creases. Or, cover the creases with a press cloth or towel.

Fantastic Folding
✳ ✳ ✳

Casual Shirts or T-shirts

Fasten the buttons and closures. Hold the shirt by the shoulder seams near the neck seam, with the front facing you. Fold the sleeves and sides back so the sleeves meet in the middle of the back. Drape the sleeves flat along folded edges. Fold the garment from top to bottom.

Slacks

Line up the seams and the hems to help keep creases crisp. Hold upside down by bottom hems; match inseams to outer seams, keeping the creases sharp. Fold in half onto a pants hanger or in thirds to place in a drawer.

Or, hold pants by the waistband and flap them several times to smooth large folds. Lay on a flat surface with seams from each leg parallel, pulling seams gently until slightly taut.

Fold one pant leg over the other, matching and smoothing the outside seams. then fold in thirds lengthwise to place in a drawer or put on a hanger.

Luxe Linens for a Tasteful Tabletop
✳ ✳ ✳

Tablecloth

Iron when the cloth is slightly damp. Use a steam iron on a heat setting appropriate for the fabric. Lightly apply spray starch or sizing to back side. Work in small sections.

Rectangular

Iron the wrong side first. To reduce sheen, use a low heat setting. To iron large cloths, fold in half lengthwise, right sides together, and press.

Refold the tablecloth with wrong sides together and iron until dry.

Round or Oval

Carefully lay the cloth across the ironing board and press the center area of the tablecloth. Working outward, iron the edges one section at a time. Visualize the cloth as a large pie (I'd choose French silk chocolate) and iron in pie-slice sections.

Folding Linens
* * *

Sheets

Fold fitted sheets by neatening corners, then folding in half from bottom to top with right sides together. Tuck fitted corners into each other.

Next, fold the sheet in half lengthwise and again top to bottom, smoothing out wrinkles. Fold into thirds. (PLEASE: If your mother always ironed her sheets, as mine did, it's up to you to stop this time-consuming practice.)

For flat sheets, with right side out, fold the bottom to the top, smooth them, and then fold top to bottom again. Next, fold side to side, aligning hems.

Tablecloths

Fold a rectangular cloth as for a flat sheet. Fold a round cloth in half (wrong sides together) to make a half circle. Fold it in half again.

Next, lay the tablecloth across the ironing board and bring the edges together to fold crosswise two more times until you have a small "pie-slice" triangle. Store your tablecloths flat in a drawer or linen closet.

Towels

If you prefer to fold towels so they're ready to put on towel bars, fold to half their width, then fold into thirds.

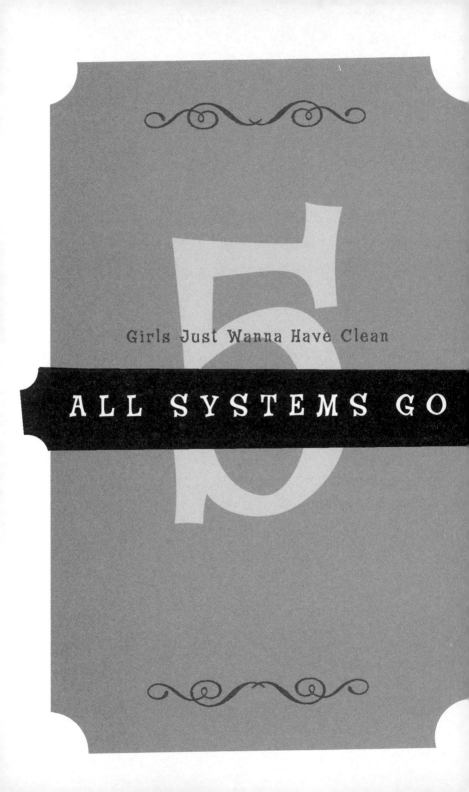

Girls Just Wanna Have Clean

5

ALL SYSTEMS GO

Systems vital to the safety of your home and family usually aren't seen, but you should become familiar with this equipment. It includes heating/cooling units, water heaters, smoke and carbon-monoxide sensors, and fire extinguishers. Knowing your systems helps keep them running well, saving you even more money to put in your kitty for that special little vacation you've been dreaming of taking.

The Basics on Indoor Systems
* * *
What Trips a Breaker?

I usually trip on toys, but overloaded circuits commonly trip breakers. They are a safety measure for your home's wiring.

Avoid overloading circuits by knowing how many outlets are on each circuit, the current consumption of appliances on the circuit, and total amperage. Circuit breakers normally trip when loads exceed 15 to 20 amps.

Designate specific circuits for major appliances. Connecting too many high-amperage appliances, such as microwave ovens and hair dryers, to the same circuit will result in overload. (Just like you do when you try to do too much when you're tired.)

A less common, but potentially dangerous, cause of tripped breakers is a short circuit. This is a result of hot and neutral wires contacting each other in either home or appliance wiring.

(By now you probably know your local hardware store clerk really well.)

Surge Protectors

Look for maximum voltage of 400 (UL 1449 rating); response time of one-billionth of a second or less; maximum surge current of 20,000 amps or more; 200 joules (maximum energy absorbed) or more; three-line protection conductors (hot, neutral, and ground); and protection for six outlets.

What's a Fuse?

(I know I've blown one in my personal life on occasion.) Fuses are sometimes used in older homes that haven't had electrical systems updated with breakers.

All Systems Go

When a fuse blows, a metal strip melts and darkens the glass on the fuse. Replace blown fuses with one of the same amperage capacity to restart electricity.

(When a family member's fuse blows, have urgent business elsewhere as soon as possible.)

Heating Hints
✳ ✳ ✳
Stretch Your Dollars

To help keep your heating and cooling bills down, consider having an energy audit by your local energy company. Usually these audits are FREE (one of my favorite words) and can turn up such energy busters as:

1. Dirty air filters.
2. A water heater thermostat that's set too high.
3. Drafty doors and windows.
4. Poor insulation.

To help keep your energy bills down, turn your thermostat to 68 degrees F during the day and 64 degrees F at night in the winter. In the summer, turn it to 72 degrees F or warmer.

Heating Maintenance

Have a professional check, clean, and repair your unit to make sure it's efficient.

Changing the Filter

This is the simplest and most effective way to keep furnaces running efficiently.

Forced-Air Systems

Rely on a filter to clean the air that moves through the furnace, into the ducts, and back through the furnace. Change or clean the filter every 30 to 60 days.

Oil-Furnace Filter

In addition to an air filter, oil furnaces have an in-line fuel filter that requires changing or cleaning once a year. Some models have a pump strainer that requires annual cleaning by a professional.

Foiled by Your Furnace?

* * *

"Rotten Egg" Odor

IMPORTANT: If you smell gas or think there has been gas buildup, leave immediately with all the family members and pets in your household. Call for professional help. Utility providers have phone numbers for emergencies.

Lighting the Pilot

(I know it's ridiculous, but I still find this a somewhat frightening procedure.) Here's what you need to do:

1. Turn off the gas.
2. Wait 15 minutes for the fumes to clear.
3. Use a flashlight to see the pilot clearly.
4. Restart the gas. (Most furnaces have a red gas-control button to push while relighting.)
5. Use a long fireplace match to light it.

If the Pilot Won't Light

For a forced-air gas furnace, look for the flame sensor (a smooth rod next to the pilot). Using a plumber's emery cloth (found at hardware stores), gently abrade the rod to clean it. Or call a professional.

If the Pilot Won't Stay On

In this case, the air intake valves may need adjusting. Call a professional. NOTE: Never stick anything into a pilot-light hole, because you could enlarge it. Never touch the igniter next to the pilot.

Squeals and Squeaks

Causes may be a loose belt between the blower and blower motor, loose ductwork, or a loose furnace door.

All Systems Go

(These noises may also be coming from your teenage daughter's friends during a slumber party.)

You can correct a loose belt by tightening, aligning, or replacing the belt according to the furnace instructions.

Ducting Seals

Check the exposed ductwork to see whether the joints need sealing. If the furnace area is warm during the heating season, or cool during the cooling season, seal both the return-air and supply ducts with mastic, found at home centers and hardware stores.

Bleeding a Radiator

Sounds like a medieval medical procedure, doesn't it? This happens when air trapped in the radiator blocks the flow of water, making the system run inefficiently. "Bleed" trapped air at least one to two times yearly.

Hot-Water Units

Let the unit cool down before you do anything. Put a pan under the valve. Open the small valve at the top with a screwdriver. Once the water flows, close the valves, but don't overtighten them.

Steam Units

Older buildings may still have these. Before you do anything with them, let the unit cool completely. You can use thin wire to ream the small hole at the top of the conical air vent. If there is a banging noise as the unit heats, call a professional.

Built-In Humidifiers

Humidity levels of 40 to 50 percent are ideal for your health and home's interior surfaces. Humidifiers attach to the air ducts of the furnace, and sensors control the humidity level. Check and clean the humidifier waterways every few months.

All Systems Go

Fireplaces
*** * ***

Gas-Fueled

Ones with ceramic logs are convenient because they can be instantly turned on and off. Fuel is provided through a gas line, and the spent fuel from direct vent fireplaces is exhausted outdoors.

For safety, insist on an oxygen-depletion sensor that shuts off the appliance when oxygen in the room falls below a safe level.

Starting a Wood Fire

(I learned this in Girl Scouts, but haven't had much chance to use it since.)

- Open the exhaust damper.
- Stack a small pile of dry kindling on the grate.
- Stack several 2- to 3-inch-diameter logs on top of the kindling, allowing air space between the logs.
- Stuff paper under the grate or put fire-starter sticks in the kindling. Don't burn colored papers—they release harmful fumes.
- Place crumpled paper on top of the logs. Ignite the paper. Never use flammable liquids. They could cause the flames to leap out into the room.
- When the paper burns, ignite the kindling or starter sticks.
- Before the fire gets hot, adjust the exhaust damper to halfway, allowing efficient burning by sending heat into the room rather than up the flue.
- Burn only hardwoods.

Safety and Maintenance

Schedule annual professional inspections, cleaning, and repair of chimneys, flues, and vents in your fireplace.

- Always use a fireplace screen made of fine steel mesh that fully covers the firebox. It will keep sparks and cinders from going into the room.

All Systems Go

- Keep mantel decorations far away from the firebox opening.
- Fire-resistant hearth rugs can help protect floors when the hearth doesn't extend outside the firebox. Never use ordinary rugs—many are flammable.
- Don't use water to put out a fire. Smother the flame with baking soda, clay cat litter, or sand.

Cooling Systems
* * *

Clear the Condensate Drain

Each year before operating the whole-house air-conditioner, unhook the drain line from the furnace and blow through it to clear it.

Pour water through the pump reservoir to see whether the drain empties into the pump. Drain lines may clog during use or freeze in cold weather.

Wash Condensing Unit

Yearly, spray water to wash dust from the condenser coils.

Change the Filter

Change or clean the air filter every 30 to 90 days.

Adjust the Damper

See whether your system includes dampers near the furnace that are labeled "summer" and "winter." In two-story structures, they send warm air to lower floors, and in the heating season, cool air to upper floors.

Clean Window Units

Change or clean filters monthly during the cooling season. Remove them from the window opening to store them.

If your units are more than 10 years old, consider replacing them with energy-efficient ones.

All Systems Go

Use Attic Fans

If you don't have air-conditioning, attic fans act as an exhaust to cool your place. Install soffit vents so the fan can pull outside air into the house.

Keep It Light
* * *

Incandescent

These have a warm glow, are inexpensive, readily available, and usable on dimmers. (I prefer this type of lighting because I think it makes me look 10 years younger. Well, make that 5 years.)

Florescent Bulbs

These last up to 20 times longer with four times as much light as incandescent bulbs of the same wattage. Compact types are available.

Halogen Bulbs

Powerful illumination comes from this type of bulb.

It gives up to three times as much light as comparable incandescent bulbs and lasts twice as long. Touching bulbs with bare hands reduces their lives; wear work gloves (let those halogens live to a ripe old age).

Dimmer Switches

Dimmer switches are great for creating a low-light, romantic mood for you and your significant other (or for when you don't want your guests to see exactly what they're eating).

Plan Bulb Replacements

When replacing bulbs in hard-to-reach places, do what businesses do—replace them all at once.

Reduce Burnouts

Lights below high-traffic areas get jostled the most, and jarring weakens the filament and shortens the life of the bulb. Replace lights in these areas with bulbs that are sold for ceiling fans or overhead garage door openers. They're designed to take shaking.

Water System Maintenance

* * *

Save Water

Reduce bathroom water use by installing faucet aerators, water-saving showerheads, and toilet floats. (You can also set a 5-minute timer when your teen starts taking a shower. When the timer goes off, go to the bathroom door and repeatedly hit a dishpan with a metal spoon, yelling, "Out, Mr.—or Ms.—Clean!")

Save Energy

Wrap the heater in a special insulating blanket, available at most hardware stores and home centers. (This is a special kind of blanket, not the kind you take a nap with.)

Reduce the temperature of the water heater when you're not home for an extended time.

Maintain the Water Tank

Water heaters have inexpensive dip-tubes that divert cold water to the tank bottom, allowing the hot water to remain at the top. If the water from the tank is lukewarm, the dip-tube may require replacement.

Flush the Tank

Flush the sediment from your water heater tank yearly:

- Shut off the water supply at the water heater and let the water cool several hours.
- Shut off the cold-water supply to the water heater.
- Connect a hose to the faucet at the bottom of the heater and run it to a floor drain.
- Open the water heater drain faucet, allowing most of the water to drain.

All Systems Go

- Turn on the cold-water supply to flush out the sediment.
- Close the drain faucet and open a nearby hot-water faucet to prevent air buildup in the hot water heater tank lines.

NOTE: Drain faucets on water heaters might refuse to close completely. You may have to have a plumber replace the faucet to prevent dripping.

- Follow the manufacturer's instructions for relighting the pilot light. Use a long wooden match to light the pilot before turning on the gas; don't allow gas to build up before igniting.

Do a Carbon Monoxide Test

Confirm that carbon monoxide isn't leaking due to an improper draft at the water heater. A tightly closed house might have air flowing out via a fireplace or vent fan, creating a reverse air flow in the water heater flue.

- To test this, turn down the water heater thermostat and allow the water heater and flue to cool for at least an hour.
- Light the fireplace and turn on a kitchen fan. Inspect the water heater flue for soft areas and corrosion.
- Turn up the thermostat. If the furnace flue connects to the water heater flue, turn off the furnace.
- Light an incense stick and hold it next to the flue opening at the top of the tank.
- Smoke should be drawn into the flue; if not, there is a back-draft problem. Call a plumber immediately.

Use Antiscald Valves

These devices prevent sudden water temperature changes, particularly in the shower or bath. They allow the water heater to remain at a high setting, but limit the water in the bathroom to a safe 120 degrees F.

Home centers stock add-on devices that can be installed. If your home isn't equipped with antiscald devices, set the water heater thermostat at 125 degrees F, or as low as 105 degrees F if you have kids, to avoid injuries.

Use Water Softeners

Hard water contains calcium and magnesium that cause residue buildup, clogging valves. Hard water also reduces the efficiency of soap and detergent.

Combat Iron

Built-up iron deposits can decrease a water softener's effectiveness. Use a liquid iron remover made for water softeners to remove deposits.

Add Salt

Replenish the salt when the salt-tank is nearly empty, filling it two-thirds full to help prevent it from compacting.

Plumbing Concerns
* * *
Frozen Water Lines

Wrap water lines in the exterior walls or attics with heating tape or insulation. For outdoor water supply lines, install freezeproof sill cocks or shutoff valves in the pipe to turn off the water supply.

Disconnect water hoses from outdoor faucets before the cold season.

Frozen Drains

Water in drains along the exterior walls may freeze. Alleviate this by leaving cabinet doors open to the heat in the room.

(This is much more pleasant to do if your cabinets are neat and not messy, with heavy items like canned corn and bean soup falling on your head—or your guests' heads—when you open them.)

Home Safety and Security

* * *

Fire Safety

Identify, practice, and post fire escape routes so everyone in your home knows how to leave in an emergency. In addition, be sure to:

- Assign a meeting place outside and make sure everyone knows where it is and how to get there.
- Close all the bedroom doors at night. Closed doors slow smoke and gases from entering, while providing time to respond to fire-detector alarms.
- Install fire escape ladders in second floor bedrooms and check existing ladders for safety.
- Store flammable chemicals, including machines with gas tanks, in well-ventilated outbuildings or special fireproof cabinets.
- Dispose of oil- or solvent-soaked rags safely to avoid spontaneous combustion. Hang or spread them to dry, letting combustible elements dissipate.
- If you use live Christmas trees, assign one person to water them daily. Dry trees pose a fire threat during the holidays.
- Don't leave stovetop burners unattended. Turn them off when you leave the house.
- Avoid hot settings when you're cooking with oil.
- To effectively smother stove or grease fires, throw baking soda on them. Never throw water— it could splatter.

Fire Extinguishers

Mount Class ABC fire extinguishers in the kitchen and garage. Select rechargeable units and have them inspected annually. Using an extinguisher incorrectly can spread the flames. See how to use one correctly on the next page.

All Systems Go

1. Set the fire extinguisher unit on a hard surface.
2. Remove the lock pin.
3. Hold the canister upright.
4. Aim the nozzle at the base of the flame.
5. Squeeze the levers.

Smoke Detectors

Install at least one on each level of your home, using battery-operated or battery-backup alarms that detect both smoke and heat even in case of power failure. Here are some tips:

- Put one smoke detector in each bedroom and in all of the hallways.
- Smoke rises, so attach the detectors to the ceilings, or high on the walls.
- Conduct battery tests every 30 days for every alarm. (Most have a push button for testing.) If your smoke detectors don't have a test button, test the alarm every six months by holding a blown-out smoking candle near the alarm unit.

- Don't mount smoke alarms or fire detectors in the kitchen, bathroom, utility room, workshop, or garage, where routine heat, smoke, and moisture could trigger the system unnecessarily.

Carbon-Monoxide Sensors

Install carbon-monoxide sensors on each level of the house. They're activated by dangerous levels of the colorless, odorless toxic gas. Assign a specific day each month to test the alarm.

Securing Your Place
✳ ✳ ✳

Perimeter

Assess your yard carefully to help ward off prowlers:
- Don't leave tools or ladders out, as they could invite illegal entry.
- Inadequate nighttime lighting makes a house inviting to thieves, so be sure you have working lights outside at night.

All Systems Go

Protect Points of Entry

Exterior doors and windows are obvious, but also consider access through attached garages or crawlspaces. Make sure you can lock these properly to thwart burglars.

Doors
* * *

Stubborn Locks

Lubricate keyholes with powdered graphite, available in squeeze tubes at hardware stores.

Fix Swinging Doors

Repair interior doors that either swing open or shut on their own by removing one hinge pin and bending it slightly with a hammer. Return the pin to the hinge and test the door.

Reinforce Door Frames

Replace short screws with 3-inch screws. This ensures a tight fit so the door can't be wedged open with a pry bar. Avoid using hollow-core doors on exteriors because they are easy to break through. Solid doors are safer and more energy efficient.

Install a quality dead bolt lock with a rectangular bolt that extends at least 1 inch into the door frame. Locksmiths can advise on what locks are best to use, and install them for you.

Secure Windows
* * *

Install locking window latches, or install lag screws in sashes, to keep windows from opening wide enough for human entry. Secure sliding windows with key locks and threshold bars.

Close curtains or blinds at night or when you're away. Unwelcome guests are easily tempted when they know what the prize will be.

All Systems Go

Provide Lighting
* * *

- Light all doorways, including the garage, basement access, and safety-egress windows.
- Install motion-detector lights over windows. (Besides illuminating burglars, it will light up those naughty teens sneaking home after curfew.)
- Install floodlights or decorative lights along your sidewalk approaches and under the shrubbery.

Take Inventory
* * *

For insurance purposes, correctly inventory everything in your home.

- Note everything, including the contents of all closets and drawers. It's great to also take pictures, digital photos, or a movie of all of your belongings to go along with this inventory.
- File receipts for big-ticket items, such as electronic systems, computers, and televisions, as proof of ownership and value.
- Keep your inventory in a fire-resistant safe or in a safe-deposit box at the bank.

Yard Maintenance
* * *

Trim foundation shrubbery to eliminate hiding places for potential thieves. Plant thorny hedges as barriers to burglars. Fencing and gates with locks or safety latches make access difficult.

Outdoor Systems
* * *

Garage-Door Openers

Garage-door openers last about 12 years. Replace units every 10 to 12 years.

Test auto-reverse garage-door opening mechanisms by placing a roll of paper towels at the base of the doorway.

The closing door should reopen immediately as it comes close to the roll.

Grilling Precautions

Propane bottles are dangerous when poorly maintained. Upgrade connectors to Type I (hand-tightened) types.

Lawn Mowers
* * *

Maintenance

Here are ways to keep your mower well maintained:

- Use proper fuel and oil; check the owner's manual for complete instructions.
- Clean clippings from the mower's underside after each use.
- Check blades often and keep them sharp.
- Replace spark plugs at the beginning of the season.
- Clean or change the air filter after every 25 hours of operation.

Winter Storage

Properly store your lawn mower during the winter. Here's how:

- Drain the fuel tank or add fuel protectant.
- Clean the deck with detergent and water.
- Check the bottom of the air filter. The bottom often collects dirt while the top is clean. (You may have noticed this kind of thing happening on occasion with your kids.)

Snow and Ice Tools
* * *

Shovels

Choose snow shovels that are strong and durable. Shovels made of lightweight materials, such as polyethylene, aluminum, or plastic, make for easier lifting, rust-resistance, and longer wear. Special coatings prevent snow from sticking to the scoop.

All Systems Go

Handles, Grips, and Blades

Here are some tips on what to look for in a shovel:

- On shovels, aluminum tube handles are lighter and stronger than wooden handles.
- Some models are ergonomically designed with large D-grips that fit gloved hands.
- Bent-handle designs reduce back and shoulder stress.
- Short handles work well in light snow. Long handles provide better leverage in heavy snow.
- Blade width determines the size of the pathway in one push. A 1- to 2-foot blade clears most walkways.

Travel Safety Gear

If you travel where snow is forecast, be prepared with:

- Blankets and sleeping bags
- Flares for signaling
- Jumper cables
- Bottled water
- Dry snacks
- Ice scraper
- Flashlight and extra batteries

Using Chemical Deicers

When used and cleaned up properly, deicers are an option to help reduce ice buildup. Here are a few suggestions:

- Use them only after shoveling. Some methods provide traction; others keep ice from forming; none melt ice. (Kind of a misleading name, isn't it?)
- Ashes, cat litter, cinders, and sand are common household remedies to keep tires—and people—from slipping. Sand is the best. The others can become slippery.
- Some chemicals will erode concrete that's less than two years old. Follow the directions on the package.
- Rock salt performs best at 15 to 20 degrees F.

All Systems Go

Snowblowers

Be sure to follow all the following safety precautions.

- For the best performance, keep the snowblower in good operating condition.
- Check the adjustment and operation of the clutch, blower system, and chute positioning before each operating session.
- Don't ever put your hands or feet in the chute.

Seasonal Checklists
*** * * ***

Fall Maintenance

- Rake leaves weekly if possible, following local guidelines for disposal; or shred leaves with a mulching mower. Raking leaves together on a crisp fall day can be a fun family project, with hot cider and doughnuts as a reward.
- Trim the trees.
- Clean the gutters and downspouts.

- Drain the sprinkler system and hoses. Remove hoses from spigots and store them coiled and flat (hanging them can cause weak spots).
- Caulk gaps or cracks in your home's exterior. (WORD FROM THE WISE—get a caulking gun. It's fun and easy to caulk with, and you don't even need a permit.)
- Clean, close, or install storm windows, or seal windows with insulating film from hardware stores. URGENT NOTE: Don't skimp here. Buy the most expensive insulating kit possible.

(The low-cost ones, once bought by cheapie me, have horribly flimsy film that flips this way and that. At the close of this project you could end up looking like "The Mummy" or "Return of the Mummy" from the "Late, Late Show," with layers of film wrapped about you. Although your kids might enjoy watching then telling their friends all about it.)

- Install low-energy light bulbs. Just replacing one regular model with a special high-energy one can save you $14-$18 a year.

Spring Maintenance

- Inspect step ladders to ensure that the rungs fit tightly.
- Test the sump pump if you have one. Just operate the motor to make sure it's working correctly.
- Test smoke and carbon monoxide detectors. Replace the batteries if necessary. (You wouldn't want to miss that high-pitched, shrieking sound when you burn dinner and company's there.)
- Check fire extinguishers to make sure they're working. (It's a good idea to have one in the kitchen and garage.)
- Make sure everyone in your family knows where the fire extinguisher is and how to use it. (Except maybe for

toddlers, hamsters, turtles, or gerbils.)

- Clean the gutters and inspect and repair loose brackets, bends, or breaks.
- Clear away dead branches and leaves. Prune trees, bushes, and shrubs. (But watch just what you're cutting with those pruning shears, and don't cut the cord from your central air-conditioning unit, as I once did in a rare "I can be handy" mood.)
- Check all exhaust fans and vents to make sure they're working correctly.
- Clean and condition your outside deck.
- Check into having a professional heating and cooling service come out and properly clean and maintain your system.
- Inspect your roof for snow or ice damage. If you see any, you may want to call a professional roofer to check out any possible damage and give you an estimate to repair it.

Girls Just Wanna Have Clean

TALK CLEAN TO THEM

"Let's Clean House!"

No matter how jovial or sparkly your tone is when you say this to your family, these three tiny words strike terror and dread in the lazy hearts of kids and hubbies everywhere.

We all know it shouldn't be like this. You work as hard as they do, probably harder. And who put Mom—or every woman—in charge of cleaning anyway? So don't get stuck doing it all. Start playing the game right. Open your mind, take a deep breath, and dive into this chapter for creative strategies that work.

Talk Clean To Them

Guess What?

✳ ✳ ✳

If someone visits your house and it's a mess, they're probably not going to think, "Boy, are these kids (or husband) terrible housekeepers."

It's a sorry tale, but in most people's minds, you'll be the culprit. Don't ask me why. I don't know.

I thought sure women's liberation, the feminist movement, or just the general higher consciousness of equality would have changed all this by now, but it hasn't. I admit, I don't know why on that one either.

So if you find yourself, day after day, week after week, month after month, vacuuming, dusting, swiping, and wiping all by your lonesome, now's the time to try something new. Because if you just keep doing what you've always been doing, you'll keep on getting what you've always gotten. (Try

embroidering that on a pillow!) Which is cleaning done so poorly that it looks like your two cats did it, blindfolded, after a four-day catnip binge.

But before we get to the strategies that work, let's quickly review the ones that don't (not that you've ever done any of these, of course. I surely haven't).

Don't Ever Ask

"Why does this house look like a pigsty?" Why not ask this? Because you'll probably get one of the following answers, or something similar, right back.

Possible Answers

- What's a pigsty?
- Pig grunts, oinking, and laughing.
- I want to live in a pigsty— it sounds really, really fun!
- I don't see anything wrong about the way it looks. I like it like this.

Talk Clean To Them

Don't Ever Ask

"What would your best friend say if he or she saw your room looking like this?"

Possible Answers

- He wouldn't care. He's a way worse slob than me. You should see his room.
- I'll just go to her house all the time and not let her ever visit over here.
- (With a pitiful look) I don't have any friends so it doesn't matter.

Don't Ever Ask

"Why do I always have to clean up this whole place by myself?"

Possible Answers

- Because we don't care if it's dirty, and you care way too much.
- Because you're the Mom and Moms are the ones who are supposed to clean.
- Because you know how to do it, and we don't know how to do it. (And they can really prove that one to you.)

Don't Ever Ask

"How many weeks has it been since you changed the sheets?"

Possible Answers

- I can't remember. Why are you asking?
- We're having a contest to see who can go the longest without changing sheets.
- What sheets?

Don't Ever Ask

"What about when you grow up? How do you think your husband (or wife) will like living like this?"

Possible Answers

- I'm NEVER getting married, ever.
- I'll look for someone as sloppy as me.
- We can just live in separate houses.

• I'm going to marry somebody really rich, and we'll have maids to clean up after us.

Winning Strategy
1
✳ ✳ ✳
Bribe Them with Something Special

It's shameful to think you have to bribe your own family to help you. It's degrading. It's shallow. It's deceitful. And it works.

Maybe your little ones have been wanting to go to the zoo or on a picnic. Perhaps your teenage daughters yearn for an afternoon at the local mall to eyeball the guys.

They may want to try on an endless parade of glittery and inappropriate prom dresses, even though it's only November and the prom is in mid-May.

Maybe your significant other would like to share a back massage and a bottle of wine. (Add the promise "without the kids" and you'll really have a winning idea.)

Offer them two hours of whatever activity they choose for every two hours of cleaning they do for you. If your house is a super-pit, offer two hours of fun for one hour of cleaning. You'd be amazed at how much three or four highly motivated cleaners can get done, even in just an hour.

Winning Strategy
2
✳ ✳ ✳
Chart the Savings

Explain to your crew what professional cleaning costs in the real world. Have each one call a different cleaning company and get an estimate for cleaning your home.

Chances are, it won't be less than $100 a month.

Tell everyone if they clean for one hour a Saturday each month, you'll put half that cost in a special bank for something fun. It could be a short-range goal like a movie or bowling, or a long-range one like a weekend getaway.

Winning Strategy 3

* * *

Make It a Game

Just a wild guess, but maybe some of the members of your family are competitive. (We're talking John McEnroe in action on the court here.) Why not use this against them? For example, challenge your two preteen kids—set the timer and see who can get equal tasks done the fastest.

Keep track of the winners on a chart. At the end of the month, cook the winning person's favorite dinner and give them a small prize, like bubble bath for a girl or a small coin collecting kit for a boy.

Winning Strategy 4

* * *

Dance Fever

This one can really be fun. Have each family member pick his or her favorite artist's fastest music.

Then, each Saturday, one family member gets to play their chosen artist's fastest music for one hour (or one half-hour) while everyone dances to the beat as they clean.

Your kids—and maybe even your significant other—might not even know how well you can do "The Freddy," "The Swim," or "The Pony." Good-natured teasing and kooky pictures for future blackmail are allowed.

Winning Strategy 5

✳ ✳ ✳

Threaten Embarrassment in Front of Their Friends

(WARNING: This is only to be done in desperate situations, like when mold is growing behind the toilet, the kitchen floor sticks to everyone's bare feet, and the dog is the main utensil everyone uses to clean up spills from barbecue sauce to rice cereal squares.)

- First, set the stage by ratting up your hair in a rooster-like, punk-rock look. Gel it. Spike it.
- Don't wear makeup.
- Put on your rattiest pajamas. Wear your robe inside out, open, with the belt trailing forlornly behind you.
- Wear mismatched house slippers. Limp a little.
- Carry some wadded up toilet tissues in one hand, because you might cry at any minute.

- Next, wander about the house mumbling nonsense about cleaning and filth and soil and how much you enjoy living in it and that it's the newest decorating trend of the future.
- Then invite your family members to have their friends over immediately.
- If they don't want to, start calling their friends anyway. Soon they'll start helping, or promise to, which is better than nothing.

Strategy 6

✳ ✳ ✳

Play it Straight

You'll notice I called this a strategy, not a winning strategy. That's because I've never heard of anyone who has used it being successful with it.

But you might be just the one who's going to put the proper spin on it and carry it through to triumph. Here we go:

1. Call an urgent family meeting. Say there will be food and treats at the meeting, to help ensure a good turnout. (That would be treats such as anything chocolate or a salty, crunchy snack mix, not yogurt-covered raisins or dried prunes.)

2. Honestly say you're overwhelmed and you just can't do all this cleaning of the house and everyone's stuff all by yourself.

3. Get their help to aid you in making a comprehensive list of weekly and monthly household chores.

4. Assign chores to each member of the family, giving the easiest to the youngest.

5. Tell them how much you love them, especially for giving this a try and helping you out.

6. Arrange for another meeting a month later to see how it's working. (Again, promise food.)

If this works, call or write me and we'll feature you, your family, and your winning cleaning strategies in our next cleaning and organizing book. I'm not kidding!

Ms. Vicki Christian
Editor
Meredith Corporation
1716 Locust Street
Des Moines, IA 50309-3023

7

Girls Just Wanna Have Clean

HOME SAFE

Comfy homes need the right indoor environment. Now that you have your act together, and household systems are going well, tackle another part of a creating a healthy home. You can arrive at this indoor comfort zone by keeping a safe, pest-free household, except maybe for Uncle Alfie—who pops up for a three-week unannounced visit every few years.

Gas Pollution
✳ ✳ ✳

Health Issues—
Suspect Your House

If family members are chronically ill, especially with headaches or nausea from unknown causes, have all of your gas appliances professionally inspected for leaks.

Consider the Possible Culprits

Low levels of carbon monoxide, radon gas, mold, lead poisoning from paint, or drinking water (even if you have a filtering system) could be the cause. You may need to leave the house until the cause is determined and fixed.

Radon Detection

Levels vary daily and seasonally. Test kits are available from hardware stores and home centers. Contact the American Lung Association at (212) 315-8700 for details.

Look Out for Lead

Kids who get adequate calcium and iron in their diet absorb less lead if exposed. A simple blood test by a pediatrician determines health risk and treatment.

Be especially alert to this issue if you live in an older (pre-1970s) dwelling.

Say "No" to Smoking

Keep it out of the house. Exposure causes eye, nose, and throat irritation. Exposed children may have reduced lung function.

Dispose of It Right
✳ ✳ ✳

Toxic Substances

Check with your city or county authorities about how to dispose of these. Some must be taken to city dumps in many communities.

Home Safe

Flea Collars

Place in paper or plastic bags and seal before discarding. Keep away from kids. Check with your vet about flea-control medications.

Gasoline

Use only containers designed for gasoline. Store away from heat or flames. Never pour down drains or sewers.

House Paint

Buy only what you need. Store in the garage or shed. To dispose, open the can and let the paint dry; then put it in trash.

Medications

Keep prescription and over-the-counter medicines out of your kids' reach. Dispose of out-of-date ones.

Pack Away Paint Thinner

Store out of reach of kids and away from heat or flame.

Pesticide

Buy in small amounts. Store locked up outside.

Indoor Comfort
* * *
Watch Moisture Levels

Humidity levels above 50 percent allow moisture to build up indoors and condense, causing bacteria and fungi to grow. (Fungi are a bunch of funguses who get together, in case you didn't know.) Levels below 30 percent are too dry, causing physical discomfort and furniture damage. Measure humidity with a hygrometer, available at hardware stores.

Breathe Easy

When used in steam humidifers, medicinal inhalants, such as eucalyptus, help clear stuffy noses. But scalding is a risk. Clean units often with a bleach solution.

If dampness occurs around a steam humidifier, turn down output volume or don't use it continuously. Don't allow nearby absorbent materials to become damp, causing mold. Stop using it and contact a physician if respiratory problems develop.

Happy Humidifiers

Distilled water reduces film and scale buildup. Change water daily in room humidifiers and clean the unit every third day with bleach or peroxide. Never add fresh water to sitting water—empty the tank and refill. Clean before storing.

Mold and Mildew
✳ ✳ ✳
Why Keep It Dry?

Quick leak repairs prevent mold spores, which can actually make you or one of your family members sick. Discard soaked ceiling tiles or paper goods. Flood-damaged clothing, upholstery, and carpets need professional attention.

Naturally Dry

When humidity is a problem in small closets, simple desiccants work. Create a bundle of chalk by tying 12 sticks together with a ribbon, allowing enough length to form a loop. Hang from a hook where chalk won't mark clothing.

Clean It Up

Mildew stains and odor are often permanent. On durable fabrics, tent canvas, or shower curtains, try washing in a solution of ½ cup liquid disinfectant to 1 gallon hot water.

Rinse with 1 cup lemon juice and 1 cup salt to 1 gallon hot water. Then wash with detergent and bleach (color-safe bleach on color fabrics); rinse. Dry before storage.

Kids' Kapers
✳ ✳ ✳

Diaper Pails

Bacteria grows rapidly in these. Wash with a detergent-and-bleach solution or antibacterial cleaner; rinse and dry.

Launder cloth diapers daily in hot water with detergent and bleach to kill bacteria.

Furnishings

Inexpensive children's furniture sometimes is particleboard joined with formaldehyde-based adhesives that give off fumes. Choose solid wood, or seal surfaces with water-based paints or sealers.

Hand Washing

This is a great, effective way to avoid disease. Teach kids to wash their hands often and thoroughly. Make hand washing fun by teaching them to sing a verse of a song while sudsing, and another verse while rinsing their hands. After wiping their hands on a towel, show them how to rehang the towel.

Safe Special Occasions

Alcoholic beverages and tobacco are poison for kids. Clean up quickly during and after parties.

Keep holiday ornaments and lights up high to avoid cuts or electrical shocks.

Don't leave burning candles on tablecloths; a pull on the cloth could topple candles, causing burns or fires.

Gift wraps with loose ribbons or trinkets can cause choking. Put them out of reach.

Easier yet, just wrap packages in pretty paper and don't use ribbons or trinkets. (Believe me, no one will think less of you for it.)

Pets

Keep pet areas clean. Keep vaccinations current and have dogs and cats dewormed with a broad-spectrum wormer. While uncommon, kids can contract their parasites.

Playground Power

Annual inspection and maintenance of equipment keep play areas safe.

Cover chains with rubber sleeves to prevent pinching.

Keep nuts and bolts tight. Fix protruding threads that could snag clothing.

Gliders can be battering rams that hit young kids. Remove them when kids under age 4 are around.

Cover the ground under and around swing sets or climbing equipment with shredded bark, play sand, or ground rubber to cushion falls.

Tame the Temp

Lower temperature of the water heater to 105 degrees F to prevent burns. Also consider thermostatic faucets, so you can program the temperature you want.

Outdoor Pests
✳ ✳ ✳

Tiresome Ticks

These little things like to fall on you from trees, so I'm always on guard in the forest. Tick-borne illnesses include Lyme disease and Rocky Mountain Spotted Fever.

Wear long sleeves, pants, and boots when hiking and picnicking. Use tick repellent on any exposed skin.

If you do find a tick on yourself, remove it with tweezers close to the tick head to prevent leaving mouthparts in your skin.

Pesky Pests
✳ ✳ ✳

Indoor pests come in through window, doors, or on pets or outside items. (Cockroaches can ride into your home on potatoes from the store.)

To help reduce pests, keep your indoor/outdoor trash containers tightly covered all the time. And make sure your windows and doors are closed and your screens are in good repair. (A nice little job for your significant other.)

Trim branches touching buildings to remove insect tracks. (No more "Happy Trails" inside your home for them.) Discard fruit that attracts fruit flies.

Natural Prevention
✳ ✳ ✳

Ants, Carpenter

Control these black pests with Advance Carpenter Ant Bait, a low-toxicity, weather-resistant bait available at home centers.

Ants, Household

Control with Advance Dual Choice Ant Bait (5 percent orthoboric acid), a boric-acid based bait.

Purchase baits at home centers, hardware stores, or online. Kill ants with a mixture of 1 part dish soap to 10 parts water.

Cockroaches, Crickets, and Silverfish

They'll consume a bait called Niban, made from boric acid.

Crickets

Place duct tape, sticky side up, on the floor near where you hear crickets. (Soon you'll have a small, dead little collection to show your friends and neighbors. Wonder if this is what is meant by the phrase "playing cricket?")

Earwigs

Trap these by rolling up damp newspaper and placing it outside exterior doors. (INTERESTING FACT: These icky little bugs got their name during Medieval times, when people believed earwigs entered the ears of sleeping persons and bored into their brains. Even though it's not true, I still avoid them on general principles after reading that.)

Keep Flies Out

Fill resealable sandwich bags with water, zip them shut, and tape them to the outside of the door. The water bags repel flies. Inside, use old-fashioned fly swatters. (WARNING: If you're single, never date a man who has a freshly used fly swatter as his only living room wall decoration.)

Stop Spiders

Capture these critters by inverting a glass over them and sliding a piece of stiff paper under the glass. Carry them outside and then release them or squish them with your foot, depending on your mood that day.

Houseplant Pests
* * *

Aphids

Yellow, stunted, or curling leaves signal infestation. (Eeeeek!) Tiny sucking insects come in many colors, winged and wingless. Wash off and spray the plant with insecticidal soap.

Spider Mites

These tiny insects are common houseplant problems. Look for their fine webs on the underside of plants. If you see webs, remove the old soil, wash the leaves, repot, and spray with a horticultural oil.

Mealybugs

These soft-bodied insects secrete a cottony white covering, distorting new plant growth. To control them, remove white masses with cotton swabs dipped in rubbing alcohol.

Scale

These soft-bodied insects suck sap. (In other words, they are soft-bodied sapsuckers.) They secrete a hard shell over themselves. Eggs form under the shell, which hatch into crawlers. (Try not to ever watch this process.) Use insecticidal soaps and oil for control at the crawler stage. Use oils to control adult scale.

Whiteflies

Found on the undersides of leaves, these infestations spread quickly. Remove damaged leaves. Sticky traps from garden suppliers hold the adults for removal.

Creepy Crawly Cereal

✳ ✳ ✳

Insects enter even clean houses on groceries, fabrics, and dried flowers. They include flour beetles, granary and rice weevils, drugstore beetles (these are beetles who shop only at drugstores), saw-toothed grain beetles, and flour and meal moths.

Flour, sugar, starch, nuts, cereal grains, pastas, dried fruits, and dry pet foods are pest favorites. Buy packaged goods in quickly usable quantities, or freeze them.

Toss outdated packaged foods. Store fresh foods in containers with tight lids. (Don't wander into the kitchen into the night, hungry, and start eating cereal from an already-opened carton without turning on the lights—you may get more protein than you bargained for.)

To control pests in your cabinets, wash the shelves with warm water and detergent. Rinse with cool water and white vinegar.

Stop Storage Pests
✳ ✳ ✳

Moths prefer dark closets, attics, basements, or storage areas where they lay eggs. Adult moths don't eat, but larvae gobble wool, fur, silk, feathers, leather. (I don't get how they live if they don't eat—maybe your kids will know.) Vacuuming removes their eggs and larvae.

Natural Pest Remedies
✳ ✳ ✳

Basil

Place fresh basil on windowsills or kitchen counters. Hang sprigs from doorways and porches to repel flies and mosquitoes.

Boric Acid

Mix boric acid with oat flour (not meal). It kills ants and cockroaches by disrupting digestion. But it's harmful to kids and pets.

Candy

Bait mouse traps with chewy candy or gumdrops. Put only where kids and pets won't find them.

Cucumbers

Rinds and pulp are popular home remedies for killing ants and cockroaches. Leave mashed cukes in areas of infestation.

Garlic

Ants and cockroaches hate this. Leave whole cloves on cabinet shelves, under sinks, or along known ant trails. Replace when cloves dry out.

Hot Pepper

To repel ants, use water, liquid soap, and cayenne pepper,

sprayed on hard surfaces, or sprinkle chili powder or cayenne along doorways. (Hot pepper causes eye/skin irritation, so keep pets away.)

Healthy Home Quiz
✳ ✳ ✳

How much do you know about home safety? Take this quiz and find out!

1. **Which type of duster should you use for pet hair cleanup?**
A. A lamb's wool duster.
B. Scented dusting powder—keeps you and your pet fresh!
C. A wet mop.
D. A feather duster.

2. **What tool measures indoor humidity?**
A. A hygrometer.
B. A barometer.
C. A humidor—and the cigars make great filters, too.
D. A curling iron.

3. **To get rid of ants, what should you sprinkle along your doorways?**
A. Stinky cheese (get rid of ants and unwanted guests in one fell swoop).
B. A mixture of ground cinnamon, nutmeg, and cloves.
C. Hairspray ("Extra Hold" works best).
D. Chili powder or cayenne pepper.

4. **Basil will repel which pests?**
A. Cockroaches and water beetles—yuck!
B. Flies and mosquitoes.
C. Ants and centipedes.
D. Annoying relatives.

5. **What problems are helped by maintaining sufficient moisture indoors in winter?**
A. Static electricity and cracks in paint and furniture.
B. Bad hair days and frizzies.
C. Mold and mildew.
D. Excess surface condensation and houseplant dehydration.

6. Mold spores and allergens can cause respiratory ailments. How can you prevent spores from spreading?

A. Grow mold-eating bacteria in your secret laboratory only at midnight, to the tune of the oldie, "The Monster Mash."

B. Don't ever wet-mop, vacuum, or dust-mop.

C. Squeegee your shower curtain or door and walls after every use while dancing to Blue Suede Shoes.

D. Repair leaks quickly. (Better yet, have your hubbie repair leaks.)

7. What common school supply can reduce humidity in closets?

A. Air freshener.

B. An open jar of paste.

C. Chalk.

D. Yellow rulers.

8. How do portable air cleaners work?

A. Air is passed through an ion misting chamber and sent to aliens on the planet Zenetar, who repurify it and then return it cleaned and recirculated for us.

B. Fans pull air through the charging area and return cleaned air to the room.

C. Air is washed, ironed, folded, and spindled by microscopic cleansers.

D. Electric impulses are used to freshen and cleanse the air before it is returned to the room.

9. Did you know plants can help purify your home's air? For 100 square feet of space, how many houseplants do you need for effective air purification?

A. 100 (create a nursery while you're at it).

B. 10.

C. 2.

D. One artificial one—daisies work the best.

10. **How long should you boil water to purify small quantities in case of a disaster or an emergency?**

A. At least 2 minutes.

B. No less than 10 minutes.

C. Until the pasta is al dente, and hold the sauce—it's an emergency.

D. Exactly 5 minutes.

E. How do you boil water?

Answers:

1. C—An electrostatic duster picks up pet hair better than the other dusters and holds it until you toss the pad or shake out the fluffy dusting head. Reserve the scented powder as a bath luxury.

2. A—A hygrometer. Homeowners can use this simple meteorology tool to determine indoor comfort levels as well.

3. D—Ants dislike hot pepper. (They also dislike being squished with the sports or lifestyle section of the newspaper.)

4. B—Hanging a sprig of basil in a doorway or window frame helps repel these insects.

5. A—The proper moisture level will help you keep your paint and furniture from cracking.

6. D—Solve the moisture problem first to stop mold from spreading. Making C a routine practice also is a good idea.

7. C—Get top marks for controlling excess humidity with a bundle of chalk.

8. B—Breathe deeply; but be sure to regularly clean the filter.

9. C—Plants potted in soil that has been mixed with activated carbon, which degrades the chemicals it absorbs, help clear the air. Avoid flowers if you're allergic to pollen.

10. A—Boiling water for at least 2 minutes kills organisms, so it is a good method for purifying small quantities.

8

Girls Just Wanna Have Clean

EMERGENCY
CLEANING PLAN

Yikes. It's one of your worst nightmares. Kinda'
like one where you forget your finals and don't
graduate from any school at all. You end up
panhandling, with a fake eyepatch and a dirty,
talkative parrot, in a smoggy foreign metropolis,
depending on the kindness of strangers. I'm talking
the nightmare of unexpected company, and you
with a very messy, sloppy house. Since I've lived
this many times, I've developed a foolproof plan to
enable you to answer the door calmly, smiling, with
the illusion of a tidy, sweet-smelling home behind
you. Read on.

First Rule
* * *
Don't Panic

Now this unexpected company could be your in-laws coming over. Your prospective in-laws. Your former neighbors who are in town and can only stop by in 10 minutes or not get to see you at all.

It could be your pastor, your priest, your rabbi. Or if you're single, it could also be a gentleman you've gone out with once, liked, and want to impress with your currently lacking home-tending skills. The main thing to remember is not to panic.

These folks are coming because they like you, and would like to see you. In some cases, they may even love you.

If you're really lucky, they may even be bringing you a gift.

Second Rule
* * *
Their Place Is Probably Just As Bad As Yours

Chances are, if you dropped in unexpectedly on these people with only a 10-minute warning, their places would be even dirtier than yours.

But with this special plan below, you'll wow them, charm them, and they'll never even notice that your house isn't all that clean.

10-Minute Emergency Cleaning Plan
* * *

STEP 1. Go grab the very biggest laundry basket or any other kind of basket that you have.

Time: 30 seconds

STEP 2. Go through only your main rooms, picking up stinky socks, newspapers, used tissues, naked Barbie dolls, and your dog's half-chewed rawhide bones.

Time: 2 minutes

STEP 3. Put your full basket in your bedroom closet and shut the door firmly, locking it if possible.

Time: 30 seconds

STEP 4. Get the spray air freshener—any fragrance will do. You've no time to be picky at this point.

- Starting right at the front door, spray liberally through all the main rooms, giving the bathrooms and kids' rooms an extra squirt or two.
- If you're out of air freshener, use furniture polish.
- If you're out of both air freshener and furniture polish, use cologne, but use it sparingly.

Time: 1 minute

STEP 5. Close the basement door, the kids' rooms' doors, and lock them if possible. (Unless the kids are inside. If they are, you can let them out first.)

Time: 30 seconds

STEP 6. Find a clean cloth or rag and some furniture polish spray.

- If you can't find a clean cloth or rag, a kind-of-almost-clean washcloth will do.
- Spray polish on the main furniture only in the living room, dining room, and den. (I'm talking JUST big coffee tables or a dining room table.)
- Wipe it off with the rag or kind-of-almost-clean washcloth.

Time: 2 minutes

STEP 7. Put some great music on your CD player or your tape player.

- For guests 55 plus, Frank Sinatra, Perry Como, or Tony Bennett is great.

Emergency Cleaning Plan

- For company aged 40-54, try Cher or Elvis.
- For a 30-39 crowd, slip on Norah Jones or Alanis Morissette.
- For under 30 guests, try Laura Love, Christina Aguillera, or anything by Nine Inch Nails.

Time: 1 minute

STEP 8. Turn off almost every light, leaving just enough illumination so that people won't trip. Grab some aromatic candles and put them in the living room and dining room and light them. (If you don't have aromatic ones, regular candles will do.)

Time: 1 minute

STEP 9. Focus on YOU.
- Go to bathroom mirror, if it's clean enough to see yourself in. If not, go to a bedroom mirror.
- Fluff up your hair.
- Wipe any major dark stains off your blouse.
- Put on lipstick or lip gloss.

- Squirt a little cologne on yourself, if there's some handy in the bathroom.

Time: 1 minute

Total Emergency Cleaning Time:
Just 10 minutes!

Extra Bonus— Extreme Emergency Cleaning Plan
✳ ✳ ✳

This applies only if the company comes 5 minutes earlier than announced, so that you have only 5 minutes or less to prepare. The minute you see their car pulling into your driveway, do the following:

1. Drag the vacuum cleaner out and put it in the living room, but don't plug it in.
2. Put the can of furniture polish and dust cloth on the most prominent table in your living room.
3. Take a deep breath.

4. Greet your guests warmly. Smile convincingly and apologize for your dirty house. Gesture to the vacuum cleaner and furniture polish and say, "But as you can see, I was just getting ready to clean the house."

Congrats—You did it!

Tips So You Won't Need Emergency Plans
✳ ✳ ✳

There's no doubt the Emergency Cleaning Plans in this chapter can work in a pinch. But what's better is if you get on top of your cleaning, and stay on top of it so they aren't needed. Here are a few tips to help you:

Focus, Focus, Focus

- As you clean, turn your phone off, so you won't get distracted with conversations until the job is done.

- Avoid another distraction by not looking at your computer in box to check out your e-mail.
- Don't leave the television on, especially on a movie station. It's just too tempting to get sucked into watching "Titanic" or "An Affair to Remember" for the third time instead of cleaning the bathroom grout.

Conquer the Clutter

Here are tips to help you avoid a cleaning emergency:

- Consider buying a tool apron for cleaning. It has many pockets where you can stash paper towels, glass cleaner, sponges, a can of furniture polish, etc.
- Pick up stray items in every room, every day, and put them where they belong.
- Have enough storage containers, files, or boxes so you can house an organized collection, whether it's clothes, shoes, past tax returns, or other papers.